THE CHEAP BASTARD'S® GUIDE TO

Miami

HELP US KEEP THIS GUIDE UP TO DATE

We would love to hear from you concerning your experiences with this guide and how you feel it could be improved and kept up to date. Please send your comments and suggestions to:

editorial@globepequot.com

Thanks for your input, and happy travels!

CHEAP BASTARD'S® SERIES

THE CHEAP BASTARD'S® GUIDE TO

Miami

Secrets of Living the Good Life—For Less!

First Edition

Dara **Bramson**

gpp®
travel

Guilford, Connecticut
An imprint of Globe Pequot Press

All the information in this guidebook is subject to change. We recommend that you call ahead to obtain current information before traveling.

To buy books in quantity for corporate use
or incentives, call **(800) 962–0973**
or e-mail **premiums@GlobePequot.com.**

Text design by Sheryl P. Kober

Library of Congress Cataloging-in-Publication Data is available on file.

ISBN: 978-0-7627-6004-6

Printed in the United States of America
10 9 8 7 6 5 4 3 2 1

CONTENTS

ABOUT THE AUTHOR

Miami native Dara Bramson began her journalism career with *The Miami Herald*'s Travel section while completing her bachelor's in journalism and history at Florida International University. In addition to co-authoring a Frommer's guidebook, *MTV Roadtrips U.S.A.*, Dara freelanced for various South Florida publications and contributed to books, television segments, and radio shows worldwide as Associate Producer for CBS News' Travel Editor. After several European backpacking treks, trips to Asia, Central America, and throughout the Caribbean, Dara decided to further explore her interest in other cultures and is now pursuing a master's in sociocultural anthropology at Columbia University. She still calls Miami home.

ACKNOWLEDGMENTS

More than anything, I credit my wonderful parents for instilling me with a sense of frugality and generosity. Dad, who brought me to my first garage sales and encouraged me to buy cheaply and give cheaply by volunteering for causes I believe in. Mom, who advises me to buy in bulk when something fits and unfailingly supports my dreams in general and desire to live out of a backpack for months at a time. Howie, who allowed me to be cheaper than he had to be as an "adult" and supports me unconditionally, which I also thank Jessica, Sam, Matt, Jess, and my other close friends and family for doing. I thank Uncle Seth for being my human history book, and my editor Kevin and agent Julie for making this book a seamless and enjoyable project. Finally, I'd like to dedicate this to Lyn Millner, for never asking what I would do with my degrees.

INTRODUCTION

There's an urban legend about a girl who was so broke one summer that she lined up Craigslist dates for lunch and dinner almost daily. (I'm not coordinated enough to pull that off.) If you hear this story and think it's a terrible tragedy, you are probably not a true cheap bastard. But perhaps by the end of this book you, too, will be similarly strategizing.

I'm not endorsing this specific scheme, mostly because that much first date talk would be nauseating. I am suggesting you read between the lines and capitalize on freebies as long as it doesn't require illegal activity or multiple awkward dates. Despite the glitz and glam in Miami, it can also be a cheap bastard's heaven if you know where to look. (And I'm not talking Craigslist.)

First things first: relative to South Florida, South Beach is not south; the Florida Keys are. South Beach, which is the southern part of Miami Beach, is actually fairly far north (northeast, rather) relative to the entire city. I say this to illuminate an important truth: saying you've seen Miami if you've only been to South Beach is like to saying you've seen New York City if you've only been to Times Square.

Miami Dade County is comprised of nearly 30 municipalities that span across the 2,000-square-mile city. Each neighborhood is distinct; Coral Gables, developed in 1925, was inspired by Spanish and Mediterranean design, which reflects in the street names and architecture. Miami Beach is a deco-lover's heaven and has its party reputation for a reason, though there are true Beach gems that shouldn't be ignored. Other hoods along Calle Ocho (8th Street) can be paralleled to a developed Chinatown or cultural neighborhood; you won't find much English, but you will find some of the best Latin American food in the city.

This is not to say that culture-filled Miami Beach alone isn't a cheap bastard's dream come true; think free beaches, happy hours, 25 cent public transportation, affordable hostels, and people-watching that's as entertaining as a Broadway show . . . though you can see those in the city from time to time too. Just keep an open mind to exploring the dozens of other neighborhoods that will likely yield less touristy and less expensive experiences.

I was born and raised in Miami, so I know a thing or two about the city. But I also give credit where it's due: a handful of Miami and travel experts offered to tell me a bit about their free and cheap favorites in the city, so I hope readers will enjoy these tidbits throughout the book. As a native, I took for granted many of the perks of the city. One is a fairly well-enforced indoor smoking ban; another is nightlife that doesn't end at 2 a.m. or earlier as it does in many cities.

MAJOR **NEIGHBORHOODS**

Think Manhattan, but not walkable. Each neighborhood has a distinct personality and history. Here are a few major ones that you've heard of or will see throughout the book. Otherwise, the term *Miami* will designate areas within Miami Dade County. See Appendix B for more resources and an exhaustive neighborhood list.

Brickell
Only recently has Brickell become a neighborhood considered as recreational and residential. Its history dates back to the 1870s, when the Brickell couple opened a trading outpost, which is coincidentally the trading center of Miami today. They conceived the development of the area, which is considered a mini Wall Street flooded with law firms and businesses. Brickell is also home to foodie favorites and outdoor shopping.

Coconut Grove
One of my favorites, the Grove, magically morphs from a night owl nirvana to a bohemian artists' inspiration. Its history dates back to the 1800s and its landscape, which is bordered by Biscayne Bay, has always incorporated the water into its character. There's a marina, bars, and restaurants on the bay and hotels and condos that are strategically situated with spectacular views. It deserves dual credit as a venue for shopping and outdoor activities that are family-friendly as well as a dreamland for drinks, dancing, and discounts after dark.

Coral Gables
Andalusia, Malaga, Sevilla—a few street names of a classy Miami neighborhood with Spanish and Mediterranean flair. Known well for its limestone

buildings and unique architecture, the Gables has no shortage of shopping or restaurants, both of which could occupy you for an entire day. Though known to be pricier, there are deals to be had, and the scenery is so beautiful that simply being there is an experience in itself.

Downtown Miami

Downtown Miami includes a slew of individual neighborhoods (i.e. the **Design District** and **Wynwood Arts District**) with distinct personalities. To avoid confusion, Downtown Miami will generally designate everything that falls in this part of town. It's been called "up and coming" for years, but dare I say it has graduated. Luxury apartments litter the landscape, but the true gems in this neighborhood are culinary and artistic. This may be the music mecca of the city, with venues including **Sweat Records** (page 10) and **White Room** (page 12).

Key Biscayne

Beach is the first thing that comes to mind. Between Coconut Grove and Miami Beach, this island is accessible from the mainland and is known well for its beaches, golf course, and waterfront activities. Aside from the scenic perks, it's close enough to prime Miami hotspots but offers a bit of solace (otherwise known as sleep.)

Little Havana

Calle Ocho, or 8th Street in gringo lingo, is the neighborhood to visit until the embargo is lifted. Even then, the Latin food in this part of town beats out any kitschy big city spot run by Americans. This is the real deal; the "Cubatown" of Miami. Signs in Spanish dominate and though English-speaking locals may gripe about it, this is a thriving neighborhood full of flavor. Food, first and foremost, along with art galleries and the nearby main campus of **Florida International University** and **Everglades National Park** (page 249) make this neighborhood a worthy stop. It wouldn't be my first suggestion for a hotel location, but it is high on my list for food and fun.

Miami Beach

For the purpose of this book, Miami Beach includes everything from South Pointe Park, which is south of 1st Street, up through the 60s at which point North Miami Beach begins. I'll list the cons first: sometimes it's touristy and pricey. Now the pros: deco, dancing, happy hours, museums galore, cultural events—the list goes on. Miami Beach is a little bit of everything and merely walking **Lincoln Road** (pages 199 and 251) or any major street will illuminate this. Talk about a melting pot: you have your scantily clad fashionistas, the super duper hip hipsters, locals whose skin is permanently sunburned, Orthodox Jews, and walks of life you thought only existed on reality shows.

Miami's Northern Suburbs and Beyond

The northern part of Miami includes a variety of neighborhoods that will typically be distinguished throughout the book. On the east side, there's **Surfside, Bal Harbor,** and **Bay Harbour** to name a few. **North Miami, Aventura,** and **Miami Shores** are a few on the western side. **Broward County,** which encompasses Fort Lauderdale, Hallandale, and Hollywood, will pop up in the book occasionally. Broward is not part of Miami, but it is a northern neighbor that deserves credit for deals that are worth the drive. The **Fort Lauderdale-Hollywood International Airport,** especially, deserves a shout out as it may yield significantly cheaper flights to and from certain destinations (and guarantees a more pleasant airport experience). Don't believe me? See what CBS News' Travel Editor has to say about FLL versus Miami International on p. 256.

The Southern Parts

Palmetto Bay, Pinecrest, and **South Miami** are three areas that fall under this category. As a whole, these areas are largely residential, but there are a slew of restaurants, scenic outdoor malls, and other cheap options that should lure you down. Keep in mind: to get to these areas from Miami Beach, for example, a car is the best way to go.

West Miami

Doral, Homestead, and **West Kendall** are about as far west as you can go before crocodiles on the highway become standard (that means you're hitting the Everglades). These neighborhoods generally serve as business and residential ones, but they will pop up occasionally in the book for specific establishments. Generally, you wouldn't trek this far west for an afternoon stroll.

Entertainment in Miami

MUSIC:
OF FREE I SING

"I don't like country music, but I don't mean to denigrate those who do. And for the people who like country music, denigrate means 'put down'."

—BOB NEWHART

If you're a rap fan you'll know the "305" (Miami's area code) from a slew of songs, but the city is a goldmine of musical talent beyond BET beats. Live music is not hard to come by in the city but like any discerning critic, be picky about who you see. Check out musicians' Web sites to make sure you're not going to see someone who sucks. Here are a few of the best venues with indoor and outdoor music throughout the week as well as festivals throughout the year.

BARS, **CLUBS,** & **RESTAURANTS**

The Bar
172 Giralda Ave., Coral Gables
(305) 442-2730
www.gablesthebar.com

It's easy to forgive this terrible name with fantastic lineups throughout the week. Live music, ranging from hip hop and rock to electronica and soul, is every Sat night and the acts are always listed on the Web site. Tues is karaoke, DJs spin Wed through Fri, and there is never a cover for any event.

Bardot
3456 North Miami Ave., North Miami
(305) 576-5570
http://bardotmiami.com

Shows range from no cover to $10 or more depending on the talent and night of the week. Their Web site and Twitter feed are updated regularly.

Blue Martini Lounge
900 South Miami Ave., Suite 250, Brickell
(305) 981-2583
www.bluemartinilounge.com

Almost every day of the week is live music at 8 p.m. followed by a DJ playing 'til the wee hours of the morning. This place also has sweet happy hour specials, including half off appetizers and drinks from 4 p.m. to 8 p.m. daily.

Bongo's Cuban Café

601 Biscayne Blvd., Downtown Miami
(786) 777-2100
www.bongoscubancafe.com

The Catch: Parking is $10 at the American Airlines arena next door.

A restaurant owned by the Estefan couple couldn't possibly be infused with any more Miami flavor. If you're in the mood for straight up Latin music, visit this joint for live music throughout the month. Check the calendar for events.

Brickell Irish Pub

1471 South Miami Ave., Brickell
(305) 381-6651
www.brickellirishpub.com

It's a sports pub several nights a week, but one Wed per month, live music is the theme. The calendar on the Web site is not currently updated so give them a call for schedules and covers, of which there should be none. Also, ask about their Guitar Hero and Rock Band tournaments, assuming you're too cheap to buy the games yourself.

Café Demetrio

300 Alhambra Circle, Coral Gables
(305) 448-4949
www.cafedemetrio.com

This Gables joint has free live music every Fri night and was originally born from owner Demetrio's knack for coffee-making. Since 1997, he's added a European flair to brewing coffee and serving grub. Call in advance for music schedules.

Cavas Wine Tasting Room

5829 SW 73rd St., South Miami
(305) 667-5332
www.mycavas.com

At 8 p.m. on Thurs is live music from various genres. The unique wine tasting room offers over 80 selections of ounce, half-glass, or glass wines. Call for lineup details.

Churchill's Pub

5501 NE 2nd Ave., Downtown Miami
(305) 757-1807
www.churchillspub.com

Almost every night of the week there's a musical guest or events. Admission is often free or as cheap as $1 and is rarely more than that. CD release parties and new, local talent also rule this place. Check the Web site for an updated schedule.

The Electric Pickle

2826 North Miami Ave., North Miami
(305) 456-5613
www.electricpicklemiami.com

Thurs night live guests may include rockabilly, swing, twang, blues, revolutionary rockers, and/or dance jazz beats. There's never a cover and drinks are half price from 9 p.m. to 11 p.m. Fri night is Disco Machine, featuring live acts upstairs from 9 p.m. to 5 a.m. Do as their Web site says: Come ready to dance!

The Florida Room

1685 Collins Ave. at the Delano Hotel, Miami Beach
(305) 674-6152
www.delano-hotel.com

Consider it a Miami speakeasy and the home of some great live music. It's elusive—there's no event calendar or listings—but it's known that Tues night is the night of choice. It's open from 9 p.m. to 4 a.m. Tues through Sat.

Fritz & Franz Bierhaus

60 Merrick Way, Coral Gables
(305) 774-1883
www.bierhaus.cc

Live music is held at this Austrian slash Bavarian joint Fri and Sat nights. Try to overlap with the daily happy hour from 5 p.m. to 7 p.m. Check the Web site for schedules.

The Globe Café and Bar
377 Alhambra Circle, Coral Gables
(305) 445-3555
www.theglobecafe.com

Saturday Night Jazz runs from 9 p.m. to 1 a.m. and there is never a cover. Band lineups are listed on the Web site.

Grand Central
697 North Miami Ave., Downtown Miami
(305) 377-2277
www.grandcentralmiami.com

It's clearly not an historic train station, but this joint features worthy live music throughout the week and many well-known DJs. Check the Web site for updated schedules and lineups.

Jazid
1342 Washington Ave., Miami Beach
(305) 673-9372
www.jazid.net

It's the longest-running Miami Beach nightclub and free most nights with ID before 11 p.m. Nightly music sets range from jazz to reggae to rock, which are updated weekly on their Web site. Drinks specials include $4 Kamikazes and $5 Coronas and tequila shots.

John Martin's Irish Pub
253 Miracle Mile, Coral Gables
(305) 445-3777
www.johnmartins.com

Not to get all political, but I'm automatically a fan of any restaurant that features photos of Bill Clinton on their Web site. The lack of cover charges and no drink minimums is a plus, too. There is live music Fri and Sat from 9:30 p.m. to 1:30 a.m. that includes everything from blues and jazz to classic rock.

Le Café Bistro
7295 Biscayne Blvd., North Miami
(305) 754-6551
www.lecafemimo.com

Live music is held most Fri nights from 9 p.m. to midnight. Performances range from world music to jazz. Check the Web site for lineups and drink specials.

Little Hoolie's Sports Bar and Grill
13135 SW 89th Place, Kendall
(305) 252-9155
www.littlehoolies.com

On Fri from 9 p.m. to 1 a.m. and Sat from 10 p.m. to 2 a.m. rotating live bands perform, which are listed on the Web site. There's no promising these are big names, but cheap drinks and a chill night are almost guaranteed.

Luna Star Café
775 NE 125th St., North Miami
(305) 799-7123
www.lunastarcafe.com

Musical guests perform throughout the week and you'll always find an extensive artist bio on the Web site. A cover charge above $5 is unusual, but rest assured that anything you do give goes to the artist and not the establishment. Music shows typically start at 8 p.m. but check the Web site for a schedule.

Magnum Lounge
709 NE 79th St., NE Miami
(305) 757-3368
www.magnumlounge.com

Best known as a charming piano bar and for its delectable beignets. Call or check the Web site (if it's up) for live shows and schedules. There's usually no cover.

Mr. Moe's Restaurant and Bar
3131 Commodore Plaza, Coconut Grove
(305) 442-1114
www.mrmoes.com

Every Fri and Sat is live music. If you get bored, you can always ride the mechanical bull—the only one in the city.

Open-Air Music

Besides the variety of festivals year-round that have outdoor music, here are a few venues that make a habit out of it. Various festivals also feature live music outdoors.

Monty's Stone Crab and Seafood
2550 South Bayshore Dr., Coconut Grove
(305) 856-3992
www.montysbayshore.com
This outdoor seafood joint hosts live outdoor bands almost every night of the week; try to plan your visit around the 4 to 8 p.m. happy hour Mon through Fri. A Miami Beach location is at 300 Alton Rd. (305-672-1148, www.montyssouthbeach.com).

Museum of Contemporary Art (MoCA)
770 NE 123th St.
In the Joan Lehman Building, North Miami
(305) 893-6211
www.mocanomi.org
MoCA is a great spot for free, weekly music outdoors. Their Fri night performances at 8 p.m. feature local Grammy award-winner Felipe

Ocean's Ten
960 Ocean Dr., Miami Beach
(305) 604-1999
www.oceanstensobe.com

George Clooney might not make an appearance, but scantily clad waitresses likely will. Live music and performances take place throughout the week. Take advantage of happy hour specials, typically 10 a.m. to 7 p.m., including half off drinks and $5 wing and shrimp specials. Check the Web site for music schedules.

Lamoglia, who is a saxophonist, composer, and arranger. Enjoy the outdoor courtyard, which even during the summer (notwithstanding rain) should be pleasant after sunset. The concerts are free and happen rain or shine. Check out the donation-based museum before or after the show.

Robert Is Here Fruit Stand
19200 SW 344th St., Homestead
(305) 246-1592
www.robertishere.com
This local favorite for produce is also an outdoor live music venue from 2 to 6 p.m. on weekends November through March. Check the Web site for performers and details.

Scotty's Landing
3381 Pan American Dr., Coconut Grove
(305) 854-2626
www.sailmiami.com
On Fri, Sat, and Sun, there is live entertainment weekly.

Purdy Lounge
1811 Purdy Ave., Miami Beach
(305) 531-4622
www.purdylounge.com

If you're a reggae fan, this is the place to be Mon nights. Dancehall is in the back room, there are live performances, and Red Stripe is $4 all night. If Purdy was in New York, it would be in Williamsburg; expect trendy hipsters and skinny jeans. Expect dance music being DJ'd every night of the week.

Soya & Pomodoro

120 NE 1st St., Downtown Miami
(305) 381-9511
http://soyapomodoro.com

Thurs, Fri, and Sat from 7 p.m. to 11:30 p.m., there is live music, which is typically jazz. There are also drink specials during this time.

Sweat Records

5505 NE 2nd Ave., Downtown Miami
(786) 693-9309
http://sweatrecordsmiami.com

The Catch: *Some events with little or no cover require that guests RSVP via e-mail beforehand. Check the Web site for details as each event is different.*

Sweat Records, another Miami staple and a go-to for the indie music scene, always has exciting events for little or no cover. In addition to the jams, it's a local hangout from noon to 10 p.m. Mon through Sat featuring an organic coffee bar and free Wi-Fi. It is generally a hub for all things cool. Check the frequently updated Web site for in-house events and affiliate events around the city.

Tobacco Road Bar and Restaurant

626 South Miami Ave., near Downtown Miami
(305) 374-1198
www.tobacco-road.com

The Catch: *Some shows are 21 and over and may have discounted tickets if they are pre-purchased. Check the Web site and/or call (305) 576-1234 for ticket information.*

Expect a schedule chock-full of talent at "Miami's oldest bar" open since 1912. No cover is the norm, but some shows have a cover that may be discounted with pre-purchase. This place gets pretty packed, so show up early for will call and good seats.

Transit Lounge

729 SW 1st Ave., Miami
(305) 377-4628
www.transitlounge.us

The weekly lineup is never ending—Rock Band Monday features $5 Jack Daniels from 5 p.m. to 2 a.m., Tues is karaoke, and other live music is sprinkled throughout the week. Buy one, get one happy hour is Mon through Fri from 5 p.m. to 8 p.m. and most events are cover-free.

The Vagabond
30 NE 14th St., Downtown Miami
(305) 379-0508
www.thevagabondmiami.com

Live music events take place regularly and are listed on their Web site. They usually start at 10 p.m. and don't have a cover.

Van Dyke Café
846 Lincoln Rd., Miami Beach
(305) 534-3600
www.thevandykecafe.com

The Catch: Some events carry a music charge per person for table service. The online calendar indicates which events have this tacked on, so check before you go.

Upstairs at the Van Dyke is a goldmine of live music on the beach. Performances take place nightly from 9 p.m. to 1 a.m. and feature a variety of genres including jazz, blues, acoustic, and a handful of international music.

Waxy O'Connor's
690 SW 1st Court, Downtown Miami
(786) 871-7660
www.waxys.com and www.waxysmiami.com

Waxy's features live music every Thurs with no cover and drink specials starting at $1. Wed reggae nights include an even better drink incentive: free champagne for ladies from 7 to 10 p.m. Check the Web site for schedules and specials that vary by location. A second and third location are at 1248 Washington Ave., Miami Beach (305-534-7824) and 1095 SE 17th St., Fort Lauderdale (954-525-WAXY).

The White Room
1306 North Miami Ave., Downtown Miami
(305) 995-5050
www.whiteroommiami.com

The Catch: Most, or not all shows are 21 and over.

I know for a fact they play more than Cream, so check their Web site for weekly schedules that feature local and international live music and DJs. Some nights have a small cover but most nights there are happy hours or drink specials to make up for it.

OPEN MIC & KARAOKE

Openmicmiami.com is the best source for open mic events in the city, but in case you're as short on time as you are on cash, here's a narrowed-down list of some solid open mics in Miami.

Automatic Slim's
1216 Washington Ave., Miami Beach
(305) 695-0795
www.automatic-slims.com

The centerpiece—a pole—says it all. Down-and-dirty dancing is what typically goes on at Slim's, but no-cover karaoke on Mon at 10 p.m. is a bit more tame.

The Bar
172 Giralda Ave., Coral Gables
(305) 442-2730
www.gablesthebar.com

From 10 p.m. to 2 a.m. every Tues is karaoke night, labeled Kara-O-King. Their happy hour ends at 8 p.m. so stock up then to warm up for your singing debut, which presumably you'll need.

Kara-O-King

This local karaoke business hosts many of the events around town. Their Web site, www.kara-o-king.com, is also a great resource for weekly karaoke schedules around town (with which they're affiliated, of course). Many of the events are free and their site even lists drink specials at the specific venues.

Churchill's Pub
5501 NE 2nd Ave., Downtown Miami
(305) 757-1807
www.churchillspub.com

Every Wed night at 9 p.m. there's a $1 donation open mic, which includes singers, songwriters, and the occasional poet.

Doral Billiards
7800 NW 25th St., Doral
www.doralbilliards.com

On Sun from 9 p.m. to 1 a.m. karaoke night takes place; you can also play Guitar Hero if you're more instrumentally inclined.

Jada Coles Sports and Music Café
2224 Coral Way, Coral Gables
(305) 456-9242
www.jadacoles.com

Karaoke is 9 p.m. to 1 a.m. on Mon. Drink specials are offered, including $2.50 Bud Lights.

John Martin's Irish Pub
253 Miracle Mile, Coral Gables
(305) 445-3777
www.johnmartins.com

Wed night is karaoke night from 10 p.m. to 1 a.m. and there is an open mic, typically attracting acoustic guests, on Sun at 8 p.m.

Festivus For the Rest of Us!

These festivals either revolve around music or feature it.

Festival Miami

(305) 284-4940

www.music.miami.edu

Every October University of Miami's Frost School of Music has a festival featuring their students and world-renowned guests. Events are held around the city and range from free to $10 and upwards. A full schedule is listed on the Web site.

Greynolds Park Love-In

17530 West Dixie Hwy., North Miami Beach

(305) 945-3425

www.miamidade.gov/greynoldslovein

The Catch: Though admission is free, parking is $10 per vehicle. Carpool! And don't bother bringing a cooler because they aren't allowed. If you're nostalgic for Woodstock, partake in this 1960s-themed hangout, which celebrated its seventh year in 2010 and runs yearly in May from 10 a.m. to 6 p.m. Vintage music, clothes, and memorabilia are the central themes of this event, which is held on the site of jam sessions and activist activity during the '60s. The event is family friendly and typically only one day long. Expect regular festival activities and a time warp back a few decades.

Heineken Transatlantic Festival

www.rhythmfoundation.com

This world music festival has run for over 20 years in Miami and showcases a variety of events, some of which are free. Although tickets for adults cost $20, children under 12 typically get in free so it's a worthwhile family activity.

Mainly Mozart Festival

www.mainlymozart.com

I bet you can guess the theme of this festival, which runs annually in June at various venues. Tickets to individual concerts are around $20 but there is typically a free concert or event at least once during the festival.

Miami International Piano Festival

www.miamipianofest.com

This event takes place several times per year and includes performances and lectures, some of which are free. Ticketed events are discounted to $7 for students with proper ID one hour before the show.

The Miami Music Festival

www.miamimusicfestival.org

The Catch: Evening events, which are typically held in bars and clubs, are only open to individuals 21 and over.

This relatively new event is growing, will take place every November, and is a place for emerging artists and bands to showcase their work. Bayfront Park is the daytime venue; at night there are dozens of clubs that host live music affiliated with the event. Daytime ticket prices are $12 for adults and $6 for children under 42 inches tall; evening performances are $10 for a single venue and $15 for multiple venues. They do accept volunteers in exchange for free event admission. Check the Web site for details.

Ultra Music Festival

www.ultramusicfestival.com

The 2010 event sold out and it won't be surprising to see the 2011 event do the same. Tickets aren't for cheap bastards; they start around $90 per day. But in 2010, organizations including Global Inheritance (www.globalinheritance.org) hired volunteers in exchange for free festival passes. Inquire through Ultra's Web site or Google "Ultra Miami volunteer."

Little Hoolie's Sports Bar and Grill

13135 SW 89th Place, Kendall
(305) 252-9155
www.littlehoolies.com

This neighborhood sports bar has an open mic every Thurs from 9 p.m. to 1 a.m., which conveniently overlaps with their lingerie show from 6 to 8 p.m. Wed and Sun from 9 p.m. to 2 a.m. is karaoke, and true cheapies should go on Wed when ladies drink free.

Luna Star Café

775 NE 125th St., North Miami
(305) 799-7123
www.lunastarcafe.com

Sat at 8 p.m. is open mic night. Sign up is from 7 to 9 p.m., and a spot is only guaranteed for those who arrive before 9.

Mr. Moe's Restaurant and Bar

3131 Commodore Plaza, Coconut Grove
(305) 442-1114
www.mrmoes.com

Every Tues night is karaoke night. The giant plus? Ladies drink free from 10 p.m. to 2 a.m.

Sunset Tavern

7230 SW 59th Ave., South Miami
(305) 665-0606
www.delilane.com/sunset.php

Karaoke nights take place throughout the week and typically include sweet drink specials like the Sing Sing Sing Smirnoff pitcher for $8.95.

Transit Lounge

729 SW 1st Ave., Brickell area
(305) 377-4628
www.transitlounge.us

Tues from 9 p.m. to 1 a.m. is karaoke night. Get there before 8 p.m. to exploit two-for-one drink specials starting at 5 p.m. on weekdays.

SCHOOLS, **CHURCHES,** & **CULTURAL** CENTERS

Adrienne Arsht Center for the Performing Arts
1300 Biscayne Blvd., Downtown Miami
(305) 949-6722

More important (and cheaper) than the national tours and Broadway performances that stand the stage is Free Gospel Sundays in the Knight Concert Hall. Every week at 4 p.m. enjoy the sounds of a mass choir and award-winning singers, such as past performer and Grammy Award winner Vanessa Bell Armstrong.

Florida International University School of Music
11200 SW 8th St. at Florida International University, near Sweetwater
(305) 348-2896
http://music.fiu.edu

FIU's School of Music puts on performances year-round at their campus's Herbert and Nicole Wertheim Performing Arts Center. Ticket prices range from free to $15 for general admission (always with deep discounts for students and affiliates).

Gospel Concert and Marketplace
111 NW 1st St. at Stephen P. Clark Government Center, Downtown Miami
(305) 375-4606

Get your Sister Act on every Fri from 11:30 a.m. to 1:30 p.m. Aside from gospel groups, enjoy dance and poetry performances as well.

Lincoln Theatre
541 Lincoln Rd., Miami Beach
(305) 673-3330
www.nws.edu

This theater is affiliated with the world-renowned New World Symphony, which puts on shows year-round. There are various free events and others start as low as $10. Schedules and ticket prices can be viewed on their Web site.

Live! Modern School of Music

1788 Sans Souci Blvd., North Miami
(305) 893-0191
www.liveschoolofmusic.com

If you want some innovative performances, check out those given by this music school, which trains children up to age 18. Events take place throughout the year and are listed on the Web site. A second North Miami location is at 2180 ½ NE 123rd St. Use the phone number above for both locations.

Miami Dade College

(305) 237-2282
www.mdc.edu

This local college boasts over a dozen ensembles of different styles; the Celebration Jazz Choir, a Classical and Jazz Guitar Ensemble, and a Wind Symphony, to name a few. Most, if not all, events are free and take place at various venues and campuses around the city.

St. Mary's Cathedral

7525 NW 2nd Ave., NW Miami

This concert series features the Greater Miami Youth Symphony Orchestra, performing everything from *Night on Bald Mountain* by Modest Mussorgsky to *Phantom of the Opera* selections by Andrew Lloyd Webber. The event is held every Sun at 4 p.m.

University of Miami

(305) 284-2438
www.music.miami.edu

The University of Miami's Frost School of Music boasts a free, year-round performance schedule that includes opera, chamber, jazz, strings, and choral music. Many performances are at Gusman Concert Hall and feature the schools' orchestra and other guest instrumentalists. Admission for most concerts is free, but double-check the Web site to be sure.

DANCE:
FREE EXPRESSION

"Ballet: Men wearing pants so tight that you can tell what religion they are."

—*ROBIN WILLIAMS*

Miami might lack some things, but rhythm is not one of them. Any type of dance with a Latin influence—salsa, meringue, bachata, tango (to name a few)—pervades many clubs, studios, and even the street music you'll hear throughout the city. It's near impossible to find a bar or club that doesn't have dancing at some point in the evening. But if you want something more formal—a dance class or lesson—there are a variety of studios, many of which offer free lessons for first timers.

DANCE **CLASSES**

Dance studios are obvious, but there are also restaurants and bars that have dance lessons (typically with a Latin flair), many of which are free and don't require signup. Here are a few of both that are reasonably priced or totally free.

Best of Dance
1501 SW 8th St., Little Havana
(786) 287-7260
www.bestofdance.com

Taking a tango class at 9 p.m. on Fri sounds strange, but it's a perfect way to start an all-nighter and brush up on your dancing skills. There's an intermediate class and a beginner class, both of which start at 9 p.m. Each class is $15 per person and includes a dance party that runs until 2 a.m.

Bongo's Cuban Café
601 Biscayne Blvd., Downtown Miami
(786) 777-2100
www.bongoscubancafe.com

The Catch: Parking is $10 at the American Airlines arena next door.

How could a joint owned by Gloria Estefan not have dancing? With any luck, "Conga" will not be playing on repeat. Fri and Sat nights are guaranteed dance parties, typically from 10 p.m. to 4 a.m., and other nights of the week usually end on the dance floor.

Boteco

916 NE 79th St., NE Miami
(305) 757-7735
www.botecomiami.com

Mon night from 9 to 11 p.m., this Brazilian joint hosts a free samba class. Get some 50% off liquid courage before then from 5 to 8 p.m. during happy hour.

Casa Panza

1620 SW 8th St., Little Havana
(305) 643-5343

Flamenco dancing fiestas at Casa Panza in Little Havana are legendary. On Tues, Thurs, and Sat there is an all-night (yes, until 4 a.m.) dance party. Plus, at 8 and 11 p.m. real flamenco dancers will take the stage and perform.

Dance Empire

12801 SW 134th Court, Miami
(305) 232-5573
www.danceempire.com

If you think you're an intermediate dancer, take a beginner class here. This place has bred nationally recognized dancers and is serious about its stuff. One-hour classes run $15, but the studio will give discounts to those with college IDs.

Le Café Bistro

7295 Biscayne Blvd., North Miami
(305) 754-6551
www.lecafemimo.com

Free salsa lessons are offered on Wed at 8 p.m., and the Web site's wording makes matchmaking seem promising.

PAN Performing Arts Network

13126 West Dixie Hwy., North Miami
(305) 899-7730
www.panmiami.org

Classes range from ballet and jazz to hip hop and Irish step dance. Single classes are $15 but multiple class cards can be purchased, which discount individual classes to as low as $9 each.

In the Club

I feel like a cliché club promoter saying this, but it must be said: dress to impress. Miami's best dance clubs are no joke, and half of getting in (on a busy night) is looking the part. Dancing at local bars, restaurants, and studios is always an option, but if you simply want to get down and dirty, these are the spots to go. Some establishments don't enforce a cover charge; others may charge $5 to $10 (sometimes more) at the door. If you don't want to chance a line or cover, consider that almost any bar in the city will have dancing by the end of the night. Check schedules and covers before you go as they may vary nightly.

Aero Bar
247 23rd St., Miami Beach
(305) 674-1110
http://aerobarmiami.com

B.E.D. Restaurant and Nightclub
929 Washington Ave., Miami Beach
(305) 532-9070
www.bedmiami.com

Cameo
1445 Washington Ave., Miami Beach
(786) 235-5800
www.cameomiami.com

Club Space
34 NE 11th St., Downtown Miami
(305) 375-0001
www.clubspace.com

Karu & Y
71 NW 14th St., Downtown Miami
(786) 488-4442
www.karu-y.com

Mansion
1235 Washington Ave., Miami Beach
(305) 695-8411
www.mansionmiami.com

Mokai Lounge
235 23rd St., Miami Beach
(305) 531-5535
www.mokaimiami.com

Nikki Beach
1 Ocean Dr., Miami Beach
(786) 515-1130
www.nikkibeach.com

Nocturnal
50 NE 11th St., Downtown
Miami
(305) 576-6996
www.nocturnalmiami.com

Opium Garden/Prive
136 Collins Ave., Miami
Beach
(305) 531-5535
www.theopiumgroup.com

Set Miami
320 Lincoln Rd., Miami
Beach
(305) 531-2800
www.setmiami.com

Score
727 Lincoln Rd., Miami
Beach
(305) 535-1111
www.scorebar.net

Twist
1057 Washington Ave.,
Miami Beach
(305) 53-TWIST (538-9478)
www.twistsobe.com

**Uva Restaurant and
Lounge**
2626 Ponce de León Blvd.,
Coral Gables
(305) 476-8111

Salsa Kings

11200 SW 8th St.
Graham University Center at Florida International University
(888) 40-SALSA (407-2572)
www.salsakings.com

Newcomers should take advantage of the $20 unlimited lesson deal for Level 1, which allows you to take as many classes as necessary before passing to the next level. If you pass in three hours or less, they'll award you with three lessons in the level to which you've graduated. Otherwise, individual classes cost $8 each with no commitment.

FOR **FREE** (FOR **FIRST-TIMERS**)

There's no shortage of dance studios all over Miami. The studios listed below offer free classes for first-time students. Some classes have limits, so call in advance to reserve your spot.

Arthur Murray Miami

1060 Brickell Ave., Mezzanine Level, Brickell
(305) 372-1170
www.arthurmurrayinmiami.com
Styles: Ballroom, Latin, rhythm

Aventura Dance

2650 NE 188th St., North Miami
(305) 466-3633
www.aventuradance.com
Styles: Bachata, salsa, etc.

The Catch: Only select styles are free for first-timers.

Best of Times Dance Studio

6255 SW 8th St., South Dade
(305) 269-0335
www.bestoftimesdancestudio.com
Styles: Ballroom, belly, Latin, salsa, tango

New Image Dance Company

7460 SW 117th Ave., South Dade
(305) 595-1115
www.newimagedance.com
Styles: Ballet, hip hop, jazz, modern, tap, etc.

Pole Dance Miami

17670 NW 78th Ave. Suite 111, Hialeah
(305) 456-4171
www.poledancemiami.com

Reserve your pole during a free open house!

Salsa Lovers

9848 SW 40th St., SW Miami
(305) 220-7115
www.salsalovers.com
Styles: Salsa, what else?

CHEAP PERFORMANCES

Many of these companies perform at various venues around the city. See the Theater chapter on pages 66 to 67 for performing arts venues that host a variety of events and national tours. Check their Web sites for schedules.

Adrienne Arsht Center for the Performing Arts

1300 Biscayne Blvd., Downtown Miami
(305) 949-6722
www.arshtcenter.org

The Catch: Parking is pricey (try $15!) in the area around the center, so try to carpool or take public transportation if possible. If you must drive, buy a parking pass on the center's Web site for reserved parking in their facilities instead of scavenging the area for shady (and likely more expensive) spots.

This is the home of traveling Broadway shows and national dance, theater, and music tours. Tickets typically start around $15 and go up from there depending on the performer and seat assignment.

Brazz Dance

(786) 338-5488

www.brazzdance.com

A new show is consistently on the calendar almost every month at venues around the city. Tickets are typically $12 for students and seniors, which can be purchased online. The company's style is a fusion of modern, contemporary, and African Diasporic.

Dance Now! Ensemble

www.dancenowmiami.org

This contemporary modern dance ensemble collaborates and performs in various venues around Miami. Some performances are free; others are as low as $15 with a student discount. Check the Web site for upcoming events.

International Ballet Festival

(305) 549-7711

www.internationalballetfestival.com

The festival is typically held yearly in September and attracts companies from around the world. Past participants have included the New York City Ballet, Brazil's Ballet Teatro Municipal do Rio de Janeiro and the national ballets of Hungary and Portugal. Check the online schedule for dates and venues. E-mail contact@intballefest.org for further information or volunteer opportunities.

Miami City Ballet

(877) 929-7010

www.miamicityballet.org

Students get approximately 50 percent off specific tickets with a valid student ID. Rush tickets, which are up to one third off prices for certain programs, are available starting 90 minutes before performances.

Miami Contemporary Dance Company

(305) 865-6232

http://miamicontemporarydance.net

This company puts on shows year-round, which range from a $5 suggested donation for their Sunday Salsa Social to more expensive events and performances at local venues.

Momentum Dance Company

(305) 858-7002
www.momentumdance.com

Student and senior tickets are as low as $12 for performances at well-known venues around the city. Momentum also hosts the Miami Dance Festival every spring, which features various events and performers.

New World School of the Arts

(305) 237-3341
http://nwsa.mdc.edu

New World is the crème de la crème of Miami's school-aged dancers. There's a high school program and a college program, both of which breed talent for professional careers in the arts. Dance concerts and local performances typically cost $5 for students and seniors and $12 general admission. Affiliates of New World, Miami Dade College, and the University of Florida usually get in free.

COMEDY:
I KID YOU NOT

"I can't stand cheap people. It makes me real mad when someone says something like, 'Hey, when are you going to pay me that $100 you owe me?' or, 'Do you have that $50 you borrowed?' Man, quit being so cheap."

—JACK HANDY,
AMERICAN WRITER AND
FORMER SATURDAY NIGHT LIVE CAST MEMBER

Miami's chaotic clash of language and culture in any particular neighborhood always seemed to produce more giggles than what I expected from an indoor venue. That changed after I saw Bob Saget at Miami Improv. I realized that the city does attract some legit, funny talent that is worth watching. There's not a huge selection, but schedules will reflect worthwhile (and often cheap) entertainment. Plus, there's plenty to make fun of in Miami!

COMEDY **CLUBS**

Aromas of Havana Cigars and Lounge
14781 Biscayne Blvd., North Miami
(305) 940-0988
www.aromasofhavanacigarlounge.com

There probably won't be too many smoking jokes, but the *Miami New Times* calls it "just like Cuba, except funny." It's a professional stand-up comedy night that takes place every Wed at 10 p.m. Headliners often include BET and Comedy Central guests. For 10 bucks, perhaps you can coerce the staff to throw in a cigar.

Fort Lauderdale Improv Comedy Club and Dinner Theatre
5700 Seminole Way at Seminole Paradise, Fort Lauderdale
(954) 981-5653
www.improvftl.com

The Catch: Some shows have a two-drink minimum and most, if not all shows are 18 and older.

This is the northern sister of Miami Improv, so expect a similarly spectacular lineup.

Hell Bound City Tattoos
254 NW 36th St., Downtown Miami
(305) 573-1602
www.myspace.com/hellboundcitytattoo

Let's be honest: this sounds like the most un-funny place ever. But an array of stand-up shows throughout the month will prove otherwise. Call or check the Web site for current schedules.

Impromedy
1645 SW 107th Ave., Kendall
(305) 226-0030
http://impromedymiami.com

Various nights throughout the week at the Roxy Theatre play host to an improv comedy performance. They are known to have free events, but entrance will normally cost you $10 general admission or $8 with a student ID. Performances are typically Fri nights but vary throughout the year.

Jada Coles Sports and Music Café
2224 Coral Way, Coral Gables
(305) 456-9242
www.jadacoles.com

On Tues (and some Sats), Comedy Nights at Jada Coles attract local and national talent as well as film shorts. If you're lucky, a promotional happy hour will include free drinks. But regardless, the comedy is always free.

Just the Funny

3119 Coral Way, Coral Gables
(305) 693-8669
www.justthefunny.com

Ten-buck tickets are where it's at Fri and Sat nights the first weekend of every month at 9 and 11 p.m. Student improv shows are as low as $7. If you really want to maximize your funny money, grab the $15-for-two-shows deal. Residents who can't get enough should splurge on the $70 annual pass, which is good for 12 months and more than 70 shows.

Laughing Gas

6766 Main St. at Main Street Playhouse, Miami Lakes
(305) 461-1161
www.laughinggasimprov.com

No age restriction and no drink minimum are reasons enough to go, but the $10 tickets and diverse lineup add more incentive. Reservations can be made ahead of time, but first come, first served tickets are otherwise available at the box office 30 minutes prior to the show. Almost all Fri and Sat shows start at 11 p.m.

Miami Improv

3390 Mary St., Suite 182 in the Shoppes of Mayfair, Coconut Grove
(305) 441-8200
www.miamiimprov.com

The Catch: Some shows have a two-drink minimum and most, if not all shows are 18 and older.

Miami Improv can easily brag about their former guests, which include Dave Chappelle, George Carlin, and Steve Martin, to name a few. But they consistently bring in new talent and attract regular crowds with locals and first-timers. Tickets range from $5 for New Faces of Comedy events and upwards for bigger names. Tickets are available on their Web site and the calendar is updated regularly.

DRAG **SHOWS**

Club Sugar
2301 SW 32nd Ave., Coral Gables
(305) 443-7657
www.clubsugarmiami.com

It's all in a name, no? Every Thurs is Drag Wars, which has no cover and a potential $100 cash prize if you're bold enough to participate. Sun is Noche de Cabaret, a weekly 10 p.m. show for $10 with all-night drink specials.

Palace Bar and Restaurant
1200 Ocean Dr., Miami Beach
(305) 531-7234
www.palacesouthbeach.com

"Every queen needs a palace" is the Palace's motto, which hosts drag-themed events nearly every night of the week. No event has a cover, including the outdoor drag shows on Thurs through Sat starting at 7 p.m. that feature several performers.

Twist

1057 Washington Ave., Miami Beach
(305) 53-TWIST (89478)
www.twistsobe.com

This is the longest running gay club in Miami, which is known for its never-a-cover motto and pure entertainment. Regular events include nightly dance parties and drag performances, drink specials, complimentary BBQ on Fri in the garden during happy hour, and special events year-round.

FILM:
PICTURE THIS

"A good film is when the price of the dinner, the theater admission, and the babysitter were worth it."

—*ALFRED HITCHCOCK*

Los Angeles and New York are the first two places that come to mind when film is involved. But think of this: *CSI: Miami* and *Miami Vice* aren't the only projects filming in the city. Film buffs are in luck: Miami has a respectable array of festivals and theaters that are alive and well year-round and have incentives (or just offers) for free or cheap tickets. For a comprehensive overview of the latest events, visit www.filmiami.org, which features Miami Dade County's calendar of local and international film events.

FILM **FESTIVAL** VOLUNTEERING

If you have the time, volunteering at film festivals is hands down the best way to see free films (and potentially get swag or crash after parties!). Dozens of festivals pass through Miami, most of which actively seek volunteers and give tickets as incentives.

American Black Film Festival
(646) 375-2059
www.abff.com

The four-day ABFF is held yearly in June and focuses on international premiers. Prospective volunteers should contact Reggie Scott with a 100-word (or less) cover letter at abff@thefilmlife.com. In addition to potential for free film viewings, inquire about class freebies and discounts—the festival features master classes, one of which was taught by Spike Lee in 2010.

Doc Miami International Film Festival
http://docmiami.org

Every May this festival features documentaries from around the world and incorporates other artistic performances in the schedule. Many student films are free to see anyway. If you can't volunteer, splurge on the Doc Fest Flex Pass for $30 to see any four films. Prospective volunteers should submit applications, available on the Web site, electronically to volunteer@docmiami.org.

Fort Lauderdale International Film Festival

1314 East Las Olas Blvd., Suite 007, Fort Lauderdale
(954) 760-9898
www.fliff.com

For every 10 hours of volunteering, you'll get a voucher for a free film at
Cinema Paradiso. Contact volunteers@fliff.com for more information.

Gay and Lesbian Film Festival

(305) 534-9924
www.mglff.com

Positions from ushers to crowd control are needed for this yearly event based
in South Beach. Attending one of two volunteer training sessions is required
before the festival. Sign up on the Web site or by contacting volunteer@
mglff.com.

The Israel Film Festival

www.mi.israelfilmfestival.com

The event, which is held every February, accepts volunteers yearly. A form
can be filled out online and questions should be directed to (877) 966-5566
or volunteer@israelfilmfestival.org.

Italian Film Festival

Miami Beach
www.cinemaitaly.com

This event, held in Sept or Oct, seeks volunteers and has a form on the Web
site to fill out. Italian film buff locals should also take advantage of monthly
Cinema Italia screenings at the Tower Theatre on the third Thurs of every
month. Check the Web site for festival and monthly event details.

Miami International Film Festival

(305) 237-3456
www.miamifilmfestival.com

Several shifts are required to acquire free tickets to shows, but the staff is
easygoing and the lineup is typically awesome. You don't even need a film
background to do this! Visit the Web site for the application or contact the
volunteer coordinator at volunteers@miamifilmfestival.com.

Member Without a Jacket

The jacket's not included but local film lovers should consider a yearly membership to the Miami Beach Film Society, which starts at $50 per member. It sounds like a pretty penny, but if you're frequenting films that often, the discounts will add up. Member status will give you access and invitations to premiers and special members-only events. Other incentives include a discount on one ticket per film at the society, discounts on all regular Miami International Film Festival screenings, and a subscription to the calendar and newsletter. Call (305) 67-FILMS or visit their Web site www.mbcinema.com.

Miami Jewish Film Festival
(305) 573-7305
www.miamijewishfilmfestival.com

This annual event attracts worldwide documentary and dramatic films. To volunteer, fill out the online form or contact mjff@caje-miami.org.

Miami Short Film Festival
(305) 586-8105
www.miamishortfilmfestival.com

Every November since 2002 this short film fest has featured award-winning shorts from Sundance and other European festivals. Monthly events throughout the year are listed on the Web site and typically have a $5 cover, but include a free drink and parking.

Romance In a Can
www.romanceinacan.com
Held different weekends in the spring in Miami and Puerto Rico, the event is a European Film Festival that gladly accepts volunteers. Fill out the application on the Web site or contact contact@romanceinacan.com.

Women's International Film Festival

(305) 653-9700

www.womensfilmfest.com

This festival runs every year in the spring and prospective volunteers should contact Ana Gomez at ana@wiffonline.org. Each day of the festival has a theme—family, women's issues and continents, for example—and it wouldn't hurt to specify your interest in the email.

INDIE **THEATERS**

There are dozens of generic movie theaters in the city but this list only includes the best of the best; the cool indie theaters with which your date would be impressed. Other theaters and show times can be found on www .moviefone.com, www.fandango.com, or with a simple Google search.

CinéBistro

Dolphin Mall, 11250 NW 25th St., Doral

(305) 455-7373

www.cobbcinebistro.com

The Catch: You must be 21 or older and arrive 30 minutes before show time.

You'll be ready to simultaneously eat and watch a movie after a day at this monstrous mall. All shows are $14.50, but matinees (before 4 p.m.) are only $10. The perk: parking is free with ticket purchase. The food is American-style and ranges from $7 salads to $15 pastas.

Cinema Paradiso

503 SE 6th St., Fort Lauderdale

(954) 525-FILM (3456)

www.fliff.com

It's not technically in Miami, but it is worth the drive to see some unique indie flicks affiliated with the Fort Lauderdale International Film Festival from August through November, as well as year-round foreign films. Admission is $7 for seniors and students and $9 for general admission. Members pay $5.

Night at the Museum

Not quite a movie, not quite a museum event. Don't miss a laser show in the planetarium paired with Pink Floyd, The Beatles, Bob Marley, or something hippie-eqsue. Shows are typically weeknights starting at 7 p.m. with shows as late as midnight. Entrance is $8 for adults and $4 for children. If you just want a straight up show, admission is included in the museum ticket price. Also, check out schedules for the Fabulous First Friday event, which features free admission for laser shows on the first Fri of every month.

The planetarium is located at the Miami Science Museum (3280 South Miami Ave., Coconut Grove) and can be reached at (305) 646-4200 or www.miamisci.org.

Cosford Cinema
1111 Memorial Dr. at the University of Miami, Coral Gables
(305) 284-4861
http://com.miami.edu

The Catch: Parking is free after 4 p.m. during the week and all day on the weekends.

University of Miami's film school shows films year-round that are both student-made and classics. Tickets are $8 for the general public, $6 for UM affiliates with valid ID, and free for UM students. For movie times and schedules check the Web site or e-mail cosfordcinema@miami.edu.

Gusman Center for the Performing Arts
174 East Flagler St., Downtown Miami
(305) 372-0925
http://gusmancenter.org

The Catch: This place is an official Ticketmaster outlet so you're better off purchasing tickets on-site (if you're not in jeopardy of a sell-out!) as online and phone orders will tack on a handling and transaction fee.

This center hosts a variety of arts events including live performances and films. Various film festivals use the space as a venue. The Borscht Film Festival (www.borscht.info) is a yearly event in November that's free and at Gusman.

Italian Film Festival

1508 SW 8th St. at the Tower Theatre, Little Havana
(305) 642-1264
www.cinemaitaly.com

The festival itself is an entirely separate event, but along with Società Dante Alighieri and Miami Dade College, they are a sponsor of free monthly Italian film screenings held at Little Havana's Tower Theatre.

Miami Beach Cinematheque

512 Española Way, Miami Beach
(305) 67-FILMS
www.mbcinema.com

The Catch: Though the timeline has yet to be released, announcements have been made that the Cinematheque may relocate to City Hall eventually.

A Miami Beach Film Society membership will get you $7 tickets. Otherwise, students and seniors pay $8 and non-members pay $10 per film. Their lineup includes classics, generally indie films, and is also a venue for various film festivals and events year-round. Check the Web site calendar, which is updated regularly.

Sunrise Cinemas

3701 NE 163rd St. at the Intracoastal Mall, North Miami Beach
(305) 949-0064
www.sunrisecinemas.com

This spot shows all the latest flicks as well as classics periodically. After 4 p.m. tickets are $9.75 so strategize your schedule based on their specials: morning shows are $6 and afternoon matinees before 4 p.m. are $7.75. Students always get in for $8 and children 12 and under pay $6.50.

Tower Theatre

1508 SW 8th St., Little Havana
(305) 642-1264
www.thetowertheatre.com

Free Cuban and Latin American films are presented frequently (and in Spanish) at this historic Little Havana theater, built in the 1920s. The event is co-presented by Miami Dade College.

Zen Village
3570 Main Hwy., Coconut Grove
(305) 567-0165
www.zenvillage.org

Films are shown monthly at this holistic wellness institute in Coconut Grove. Likewise, expect something earthy or spiritual.

UNDER **THE** STARS

It's a bummer that most of these outdoor movies aren't technically in Miami, but if you're a cheap bastard with brains, you'll realize that the gas (or transportation) money spent to get there is still less than an indoor movie in Miami. Plus, who doesn't love a film under the stars?

Andiamo Brick Oven Pizza
5600 Biscayne Blvd., Downtown Miami
(305) 762-5751

Did your mouth just water? An outdoor flick and outstanding pizza might be among the best duos ever. An outdoor projection screen is usually fixed on a sports station but occasionally features movies. Viewing is always free; sadly, the food is not. The site is a historic landmark, which features picnic tables for seating. If you're a true multitasker, get your car washed and detailed while you're there.

The Fort Lauderdale Swap Shop
3291 West Sunrise Blvd., Fort Lauderdale
(954) 791-7927
www.floridaswapshop.com

Flea market by day, World's Largest Drive-In by night. Since the 1960s the site has attracted shoppers and film buffs and now has 14 screens that play a variety of films. Admission is $5 for adults, $1 for children ages 5 to 11, and free for children under 5. Check the Web site for schedules.

Hollywood Anniversary Park
Hollywood Blvd. and 20th St., Hollywood
(954) 921-3274
www.hollywoodfl.org

On the second Fri of every month, the city shows foreign films from countries around the world starting at sunset. It's a bit of a drive from Miami, but admission is free and an indoor venue (the Hollywood Art and Cultural Center) is available during the rainy and hurricane season. Check the Web site for the venue where it will be held.

Maroone Moonlight Movies at Weston Regional Park
20200 Saddle Club Rd.
at the Weston Regional Park, Weston
(954) 389-4321
www.westonfl.org

This is another not-quite-Miami site, but if you're already in the northern part of the city, it's worth the 40-minute drive for free family-friendly flicks. Every Sat night at 7:30 p.m. from late October to late April, the city welcomes locals to bring chairs and blankets to the site. Check the Web site for schedules.

Maroone Moonlight Movies at Huizenga Plaza
Huizenga Plaza at Andrews Avenue and Las Olas Boulevard Fort Lauderdale
(954) 463-6574
www.fliff.com/moonlight

Classics Under the Stars is the movie series sponsored by local car dealership Maroone. Start time is typically around sunset but see the Web site for schedule details. And don't fret; all viewings are free.

Movies on the Green

1177 Kane Concourse at 96th Street and West Bay Harbor Drive, Bay Harbor Islands
(786) 355-7785
www.bayharborislands.org

Indie and foreign films are shown outdoors during sunset on the second Sat of every month. Musicians and speakers relating to the film often make appearances before or after the event, which is free and offers free parking.

Upper Eastside Garden

7244 Biscayne Blvd., North Miami
(305) 984-3231
www.uppereastsidegarden.com

Every Thurs at 8 and 10 p.m. the garden opens its doors for showings of all sorts of films ranging from foreign to contemporary. Admission is $7, which sounds steep, but it includes a bag of popcorn, a drink, and seating paraphernalia (mat or seat or whatever is available!) Check the Web site for updated schedules.

SPECTATOR SPORTS:
LET THE GAMES BEGIN!

"Although golf was originally restricted to wealthy, overweight Protestants, today it's open to anybody who owns hideous clothing."

—DAVE BARRY

Within steps of the airport exit (or even before it) you're likely to see a handful of Miami sports paraphernalia: University of Miami, Florida Gators, Florida State Seminoles, Marlins, the list goes on.

Miami's sports rivalry may not be as intense as New York City, which has been known to instigate serious brawls based on a Mets or Yankees logo, but it is the home of some unique sports including stock car racing, jai alai, and horse racing. Check Ticketmaster for tickets if you don't want to schlep to the stadium box office.

BASEBALL

The season runs from around late February through May or June. Check schedules for game dates.

Florida International University
11491 SW 17th St.
FIU Baseball Stadium, Sweetwater area
(305) 348-4263
www.fiusports.com

Make no doubt about it, South Florida is buzzing about FIU baseball. In 2010, the Golden Panthers clinched their first Sun Belt Conference Tournament championship in over a decade and there's no reason to believe the team can't claw their way back to the top in the future. Call the University Credit Union Box Office or go on www.ticketmaster.com to buy tickets, which are $7 per game; $5 for alumni, staff, children, and seniors; and free for students with valid ID.

Florida Marlins
2269 NW 199th St.
Dolphin Stadium, North Miami Beach
(305) 623-6200
http://florida.marlins.mlb.com

After winning two World Series in their short 17-year existence, the Marlins have a strong core of players and many successful seasons ahead of them. Aside from a solid team, they also have a new state-of-the-art stadium set to open in 2012. Tickets range from $5 to $50 and the box office is open Mon through Fri from 8:30 a.m. to 5:30 p.m. as well as pre- and post-games.

Miami Hurricanes
6201 San Amaro Dr.
Alex Rodriguez Park at Mark Light Field, Coral Gables
(800) GO-CANES
http://hurricanesports.cstv.com

The Jim Morris era, with two national championship titles in 1999 and 2001, garnered lots of support for this already-popular team. Even cheap bastards can enjoy the action with tickets starting as low as $9 for students and seniors. Regular tickets are $10 per game; if you want to splurge on a field box, it'll set you back $20 per person. Look out for star 'Canes who may become great at the professional level, such as All-Star left fielder Ryan Braun.

BASKETBALL

Basketball season runs from about November to March of each year.

Florida International University
11200 SW 8th St.
FIU Stadium, Sweetwater area
(305) FIU-GAME
www.fiusports.com

All-time NBA great Isiah Thomas recently took over as head coach of FIU basketball after a disappointing run as the shot-caller for the New York Knicks both on and off the court. Whether or not he succeeds at the college level is anyone's guess, but you can be assured it'll be fun to watch. Students always get in free and individual adult tickets are $7. Children under 12 pay $5, as do seniors over 55.

Miami Heat
American Airlines Arena, Downtown Miami
(786) 777-1000
www.nba.com/heat

Surfing and Scalping

Craigslist (www.craigslist.org) is one option when it comes to ticket hunting. Another site to try is www.stubhub.com. The game is like any other; last minute hunting will either yield great discounts for ticket holders desperate to get any money at all or outrageous prices if the buying demand is high. Either way, it's a worthwhile option to explore. As with any online transaction, buyer should beware. Scalping tickets at the venue is always a crap shoot, but it's been done successfully. If you plan to do it, bring cash, patience, and sanity.

Any team with a president nicknamed "the godfather" is a team to follow. Pat Riley recently orchestrated a deal bringing the hoops triumvirate of Dwayne Wade, Lebron James, and Chris Bosh together to sunny Miami in the hopes of creating a championship powerhouse for years to come. During the October through April season, most games begin at 7:30 p.m. and tickets sometimes go for under $20. The box office is open Mon through Fri from 10 a.m. to 5.p.m. and until 8 p.m. on game nights.

Miami Hurricanes
(305) 284-2263
http://hurricanesports.cstv.com

Miami's basketball program may not be as well-regarded as its gridiron counterpart, but Hurricanes Coach Frank Haith has built a solid team during his tenure that should have a good shot of obtaining the ACC crown. Tickets for all games begin at $10 and can be purchased at HurricaneSports.com or Ticketmaster or by calling the ticket office.

FOOTBALL

The season runs September through December and unsurprisingly attracts the most fans.

Florida International University
11200 SW 8th St.
FIU Stadium, Sweetwater area
(305) FIU-GAME
www.fiusports.com

If you're a sports fan, you'll undoubtedly remember the game when FIU and UM got into a fight on the field. If you hope to relive this, snag a ticket at the box office. But expect a bit more—Coach Mario Cristobal has uplifted the program's reputation, especially from the one-win season in 2007. Student guest passes are $15 per game; students get in for free.

Miami Dolphins
2269 NW 199th St.
Dolphin Stadium, Miami Gardens
(305) 620-2578
www.miamidolphins.com

Weathering a Super Bowl draught lasting just under four decades, it may be time for the Miami Dolphins, equipped with star receiver Brandon Marshall, to be a winning team again. The Dolphins' season runs from September to

December and tickets typically start around $20. The box office is open from 8:30 a.m. to 5:30 p.m., Mon through Fri.

Miami Hurricanes

(305) 284-2263
http://hurricanesports.cstv.com

Established back in the 1920s, the Hurricanes have come a long way in cementing their college football legacy by obtaining two Heisman trophies and a spot in the Hall of Fame. Tickets can be purchased via Ticketmaster and vary by event and it's worth it: according to sports experts Coach Randy Shannon may be grooming another team of national champions.

HORSE **RACING**

Gulfstream Park Casino and Racing

US 1 and Hallandale Beach Blvd., Hallandale Beach
(305) 931-7223
www.gulfstreampark.com

Gulfstream opened in 1939 and has hosted a variety of high-profile betting games and races over the years. In 2008, famed horse Big Brown won the $1 million Florida Derby and went on to conquer Kentucky. Admission and parking are free, but betting is not. The only cover you'll incur is $20 after 10 p.m. from Thurs through Sat for the venue's dance club (which is not why you're going here anyway!). Also utilize the XpressBet (www.xpressbet .com) site for local tournaments.

ICE **HOCKEY**

This is one South Florida sport that's guaranteed to give you reprieve from the heat. The season typically runs October through April, but check schedules for pre-season and practice tickets, too.

Dancing on Ice

On Fri, Sat, and Sun, why not combine a night out dancing with . . . skating? Yes! Kendall Ice Arena hosts an on-ice dance party with a live DJ. Admission is $11 per person with skates and $9 if you bring your own. If you arrive before 8 p.m. it's only $6 per person for admission and $9 including skate rental. Contact www.kendallicearena.com or (305) 386-8288. The venue is located in Kendall at 10355 Hammocks Boulevard.

Florida Panthers

1 Panther Parkway at the Bank Atlantic Center, Fort Lauderdale
(954) 835-7000
http://panthers.nhl.com

Missing various consecutive playoffs hasn't given the Panthers the greatest reputation, but if you're a hockey fan in South Florida, you don't have many other options. The best place to start is the Panther Ticket Exchange (https://teamexchange.ticketmaster.com), which is a legit ticket-trading source for tickets to these games and typically yields cheaper tickets.

JAI ALAI

Jai Alai Fronton

3500 NW 37th Ave., Miami
(305) 633-6400
www.fla-gaming.com

The Catch: Children under 16 are not admitted, with the exception of special events.

Jai what? Jai alai! Pronounced hi-lie, this Spanish-origin game is a sister to lacrosse. The games are held at the Miami-based stadium. Best of all, admission is $1 and reserved games are $2. Betting is accessible online before game day and on-site.

NASCAR

Homestead Miami Speedway

1 Speedway Blvd., Homestead
(305) 230-5000 or (866) 409-RACE (7223)
www.homesteadmiamispeedway.com

If you're a NASCAR junkie, this will be your heaven. One ticket source is www.racetickets.com, or check the speedway Web site for more information. Many events are free, but you'll pay the price for NASCAR events, which usually start at $50 per ticket. Matinees occur daily except Tues at 12 p.m. and are held at 1 p.m. on Sun. Another option is Fri and Sat evenings at 7 p.m.

GET **IN** THE **GAME**

Various local leagues are open to adults who don't just want to sit in the stands. A few such options are listed below. Also check with your local park, as they typically have leagues year-round. Sportsvite (http://miami.sports vite.com) is also a good site for searching leagues in your neighborhood.

Florida Adult Softball

www.floridaadultsoftball.com

This official site for adult softball in Florida offers schedules and resources for current and prospective players.

The Miami Sport and Social Club

(800) 497-1852
http://tmssc.playcoed.com

A free sign-up and league search makes getting involved in local teams a cinch.

South Florida Sports League

(786) 210-SFSL (7375)

www.sfsl.org

Youth and adult programs are available through this site. Small fees (i.e. $200 for an adult flag football season) may apply.

TOURNAMENTS & TRIATHLONS

Another option for getting active: marathons, triathlons, and walkathons are community events that are participatory and typically include festivities and entertainment and are often free. Whether you're an activist of a cause, are in it for the free swag, or want to challenge your physical self, there are plenty of events like this year-round. Run Miami is a great resource for all types of running-related events in the Miami area. Many of the events raise money for a cause and have a small (but tax-deductible!) registration fee. Below are a few of the biggest events and freebies to capitalize on, but also check www.runmiami.com for updated schedules.

Grove Slam Dolphin Tournament

(305) 461-2700

www.groveslam.com

There's no shortage of fishing tournaments in Miami, but this one is particularly suited for cheap bastards as there's a tab on the Web site specifically dedicated to "Free Stuff." Cash prizes are available for catches and free alcohol (with ID, of course!) is served as the event venue.

Nautica South Beach Triathlon

www.southbeachtri.com

This event is held in April and includes a free public component in addition to the race itself. Nutrition and exercise clinics are available as well as festival-esque area for families and supporters.

Publix Family Fitness Weekend
www.familyfitnessweekend.com

The triathlon is the main event of this yearly fitness weekend in May, but there are also family friendly activities and walkathon opportunities available for those who want to participate but aren't quite fit enough for the whole shebang.

SPOKEN WORD:
FREE SPEECH

"The human brain starts working the moment you are born and never stops until you stand up to speak in public."

—AMERICAN ACTOR GEORGE JESSEL, 1898–1981

Miamians are not afraid to speak their minds, and the plethora of events available in the city illuminates this. There's no shortage of festivals and nightly affairs that allow you to express yourself for a few bucks, and sometimes for free. If all else fails and you can't afford therapy, pour your heart out at an open mic.

FOR **POETS** WHO **DON'T** KNOW **IT**

I can't guarantee that you will meet your future spouse at one of these events, but I can guarantee some form of entertainment, be it witnessing true talent or imagining you are actually experiencing something comical. Either way, this is a great outlet for budding poets (hopefully those who do know it) and for those wanting to get feedback on their work. Many of these events are well attended by students in the community.

Churchill's Pub
5501 NE 2nd Ave., Downtown Miami
(305) 757-1807
www.churchillspub.com

This Miami staple has an open mic almost every Wed night around 9 p.m. for a $1 donation. Singers and songwriters rule the lineup, but poets are welcome, too. Arrive early for signup and check their often-updated Web site for monthly events.

Cielo Garden and Supperclub
3390 Mary St., Coconut Grove
(305) 446-9060
www.myspace.com/cielorestaurant

The Bohemia Room at this Coconut Grove joint becomes a poetry paradise one night a week. Professional poets and neophytes alike can participate in this weekly Tues ritual at 8 p.m.

Literary Café and Poetry Lounge

1350 NE 125th St., North Miami
(305) 981-4724
www.myspace.com/literarycafepoetrylounge

Local poets flock to this venue for open mic nights and slams throughout the week. Check the Web site for schedules.

Luna Star Café

775 NE 125th St., North Miami
(305) 799-7123
www.lunastarcafe.com

The Catch: There is a $7 minimum (cash only) on live performance nights and reservations are not accepted. Luna's open mic and poetry nights have run for over a decade and welcome poetry, music, comedy, storytelling and other arts performances. Sign up is typically 7 p.m. to 9 p.m. and performances begin at 8 p.m. Check the Web site for updated schedules and performances throughout the week.

AUTHOR **APPEARANCES** & **BOOK** DISCUSSIONS

When a book tour is scheduled, there are a few cities, aside from New York, Boston, and Los Angeles that are absolutely and always included for public relations purposes; Miami is one of them. If a book you're excited about is coming out, check the author's Web site for a book tour schedule. You'll be surprised how many authors visit Miami. Check the schedules for some of the more popular venues below—the big chains like Barnes and Noble and Borders as well as popular specialty Miami stores including Books and Books.

If all else fails, remember that the Miami Book Fair International is one of the most well attended events in the country, and popular and well-known authors are guaranteed to make an appearance.

Barnes and Noble
18711 NE Biscayne Blvd., Aventura
(305) 935-9770
www.barnesandnoble.com

The Catch: Depending on the popularity of the author, these events can fill up quickly. Show up early to snag a seat.

This national chain hosts a variety of book talks and author appearances year-round. Check the Web site for details; events are usually, if not always, free. Other locations are at 152 Miracle Mile, Coral Gables (305-446-4152); 12405 North Kendall Dr., South Dade (305-598-7727); and 5701 Sunset Dr., Suite 196 at Sunset Place, South Miami (305-662-4770).

Book Discussion Group
9101 SW 97th Ave.
Kendall Branch Library, Kendall
(305) 279-0520
http://knbook.pbworks.com

On the fourth Sat of every month at 10:30 a.m., this branch of the Miami Dade Public Library welcomes an adult book discussion group. Titles for upcoming events are listed on the Web site. Of course, participation is free.

Books and Books
9700 Collins Avenue, Bal Harbour
(305) 864-4241
www.booksandbooks.com

This legendary Miami bookstore has hosted President Bill Clinton, among other famous authors, at their locations around Miami. Art, design, fashion, and architecture are their specialties, but their extensive international magazine collection alone is reason to visit. Free events are scheduled almost daily; an up-to-date schedule is on their Web site. This venue also hosts book clubs for adults and children. Two other locations are at 265 Aragon Ave., Coral Gables (305-442-4408) and 927 Lincoln Rd., Miami Beach (305-532-3222).

The Bookstore in the Grove
2911 Grand Ave., Coconut Grove
(305) 443-2855
www.thebookstoreinthegrove.com

Their Young Professionals Book Club meets once a month, usually at 8 p.m., at the bookstore. Check the Web site for details and the current book. Membership is free and all you have to do to join is show up to a meeting, hopefully having read the book.

Borders Books and Music
11401 NW 12th Street Suite 512 at Dolphin Mall, Miami
(305) 597-8866
www.borders.com

The Catch: *Just like Barnes and Noble, these events can fill up quickly depending on the author. Be sure to arrive early to grab a seat!*

This is yet another national staple that hosts free events year-round. Check the Web site for an updated calendar and other locations.

Miami Beach Botanical Garden Book Club
2000 Convention Center Dr., Miami Beach

The Catch: *BYO food and drinks.*

Natural environments, unsurprisingly, are the theme of this book club. It meets on the last Tues of each month at 12:30 p.m. and is free for all attendees.

Miami Book Fair International
Downtown Miami
www.miamibookfair.com

The Catch: *While the outdoor fair itself is free, there is sometimes a ticket requirement or a fee for private author events.*

This November event is a no-brainer for book fans who want to see their favorite authors speak. This fair typically attracts some of the biggest names and has an extensive lineup of talks throughout the event.

THEATER:
FREE SHOW

"Most convicted felons are just people who were not taken to museums or Broadway musicals as children."

—AMERICAN PLAYWRIGHT PAUL RUDNICK UNDER HIS PSEUDONYM LIBBY GELMAN-WAXNER

Miami isn't thought of as a theater city, but there is a ton of budding talent that thespians and theater lovers should take advantage of. Regional theater is particularly big and there's no shortage of up-and-coming companies that are performing innovative work throughout the year. A few theater resources include South Florida Theatre (www.southfloridatheatre.com) and Cultural Connection (culturalconnection.org), both of which list some of the most updated schedules and information on performances and tickets around the city. Both have ticket incentives and mailing lists, which any theater buff in the region should join.

Don't forget about some of the giant performing arts centers; although they are not geared to theater specifically or exclusively, they often host traveling Broadway shows and reputable arts performances from all over the globe. Check Ticketmaster (www.ticketmaster.com) for one of the most comprehensive theater and arts tickets listings.

USHERING **FOR** INCENTIVES

Although Miami doesn't boast as many volunteer ushering opportunities as other large cities—the bright lights of New York City come to mind—there are a few advertised options available. Don't be shy asking other companies or establishments if they have a volunteer program.

Adrienne Arsht Center for the Performing Arts
1300 Biscayne Blvd., Downtown Miami
(305) 949-6722
www.arshtcenter.org

The center has a volunteer program seeking ushers, tour guides, and office assistants, among other positions. The big plus is that a variety of performances, including traveling Broadway productions, take place at this site. So think of volunteering here as a one-stop shop for all sorts of arts incentives. Mandatory orientations for volunteers are held in the Sanford and Dolores Ziff Ballet Opera House on Sat at 10 a.m. and Mon at 6 p.m. Incentives may include tickets and discounts.

Ground Up and Rising, Inc.

Little Stage Theater
2100 Washington Ave., Miami Beach
(305) 529-6233
http://groundupandrising.org

Professional theater company Ground Up and Rising offers ushering and volunteer opportunities throughout the year. Ticket incentives are offered as compensation. Call or e-mail info@groundupandrising.org for more information.

Shakespeare Miami

The Barnacle Historic State Park
3485 Main Hwy., Coconut Grove
www.shakespearemiami.com

Although most of their performances are already free, you can get involved with this event and perhaps build a resume for others. Contact miamishakes@gmail.com for more information.

FREE & VERY CHEAP SEATS

Here are a few events that take place throughout the year and offer a place for theater fans to enjoy a variety of performances at deeply discounted (or free!) prices.

Churchill's Pub

5501 NE 2nd Ave., Downtown Miami
(305) 757-1807
www.churchillspub.com or www.myspace.com/theatredeunderground

The Catch: Most drink specials, including $2.50 well drinks and discounted pitchers, end at 9 p.m. so get there a bit early to take advantage of these deals.

Theatre de Underground is an experimental theater project on Mon at 9 p.m. Acts typically include music, comedy, poetry, and art, but all performances are welcome. There's a $5 cover for this specific event.

Free Night of Theater
Various venues
(212) 609-5900
www.freenightoftheater.net

Perhaps it should be called Free Nights, instead. For about two weeks every October, theaters across the region open their doors for free performances. Past years have included over 700 theater companies in over 130 cities for over 2,000 performances and nearly 65,000 guests. Tickets and schedules can be viewed on the Web site.

Ground Up and Rising, Inc.
Little Stage Theater
2100 Washington Ave., Miami Beach
(305) 529-6233
http://groundupandrising.org

This professional theater company hosts free Shakespeare in the Park performances yearly. Check the Web site for details on venue and schedules.

Shakespeare Miami
The Barnacle Historic State Park
3485 Main Hwy., Coconut Grove
www.shakespearemiami.com

The Catch: BYO blanket or chairs as the performance is outdoors.

All performances take place at the Barnacle and are free and open to the public. Check the Web site for upcoming show schedules.

South Florida Theatre Festival

This festival is typically held from March to May yearly and includes performances, lectures, staged readings, and workshops. The 2010 festival included 37 theaters, over 40 shows, and more than 500 performances. Check the Web site for details at sffestival.theatermania .com or call (866) 811-4111.

COMMUNITY & UNIVERSITY THEATER

If you've seen a high school production and a Broadway show, consider these venues somewhere along that broad spectrum. The University of Miami, for example, is known for having a stupendous theater program, so the quality of the set and actors may be closer to the Broadway end. Just keep in mind: students and "the community" are not necessarily professionals, though perks include lower prices and unique performances.

Art South Performing Arts Center
240 North Krome Ave., Homestead
(305) 247-9406
www.artsouthhomestead.org

This artist community has various performances year-round that cost $15 for adults and $10 for students and seniors.

Broadway Musical Theatre
201 Crandon Blvd., Apartment 638, Key Biscayne
(786) 223-9663
www.broadwaymusicaltheatre.com

Student productions have included *Thoroughly Modern Millie, Seussical,* and *Annie.* Tickets typically start at $10 and are between that and $20.

Herbert and Nicole Wertheim Performing Arts Center
University Park Campus
11200 SW 8th St., Sweetwater area
(305) 348-2895
www.wertheim.org

Florida International University's Theatre Department performs throughout the school year. Tickets are around $12 for adults and $10 for students and seniors.

Jerry Herman Ring Theatre
Alvin Sherman Family Stage
1312 Miller Dr., Coral Gables
(305) 284-3355
www.miami.edu/ring

The University of Miami's Ring Theatre frequently showcases widely known productions, including *Urinetown* and *Hedda Gabler* in the 2010–2011 season.

Jewish Cultural Arts Theatre (J-CAT)
18900 NE 25th Ave., North Miami Beach
(305) 932-4200 x 130
www.jcctheatre.com

The Jewish Cultural Arts Theatre at the JCC sells student and senior tickets for $12 and adult tickets for $20. Front row tickets are $27. Recent productions have included *Charlotte's Web*, *Little Shop of Horrors*, and *Doubt*.

Main Street Players
6766 Main St., Miami Lakes
(305) 558-3737
www.mainstreetplayers.com

Cat on a Hot Tin Roof and *Cabaret* were among recent productions. Tickets are $20 for adult tickets, $15 for senior tickets, and $15 for students with proper ID.

Miami Children's Theater
Venue changes per show
(305) 274-3595
www.miamichildrenstheater.com

This theater company was formed in 1996 and showcases productions and training programs for children and young adults from ages 3 to 19. Most productions are $15 per regular adult ticket and $12 for children, seniors, and students.

New World School of the Arts
(305) 237-3341
http://nwsa.mdc.edu

This performing arts school includes high school and college level students who display their work throughout the year for the public at various venues around the city. Show tickets are available on the Web site. Tickets usually cost $12 for general adult admission and $5 for students and seniors.

PAN Performing Arts Network

13126 West Dixie Hwy., North Miami
(305) 899-7730
www.panmiami.org

PAN offers all types of classes and hosts performances throughout the year. There's typically one large production per year, which offers tickets for $22 for general adult admission and $15 for students and seniors. Other smaller performances throughout the year are less expensive. Call or check the Web site for details and schedules.

Pinecrest Repertory Theatre Company

11000 Red Rd., Pinecrest
(305) 378-8239
www.pinecrestrep.org

The Catch: Tickets are typically cash only at the door.

Shows normally take place on Sat and Sun at 2 p.m. Recent productions have included *Oleanna* and *A Talk In The Park*. Tickets are $12 for students and seniors and $15 for adults.

The Playground Theater

9806 NE 2nd Ave., Miami Shores
(305) 751-9550
www.theplaygroundtheatre.com

The (good) Catch: Local organization The Parent Academy occasionally offers free tickets for performances at this venue. Call (305) 995-1207 for required reservations and more information.

Kid-friendly performances have included *Alice's Adventures in Wonderland* and *Pluft, The Little Ghost*. Call (305) 995-1207 for required reservations and more information. Ticket prices are $15 per person for adults, $5 for children, and $10 per person for groups of 20 or more.

Prometeo Theatre

Florida Center for the Literary Arts at Miami Dade College
300 NE 2nd Ave., Room 1101, Downtown Miami
(305) 237-3262 or (305) 237-3940
www.prometeotheatre.com

Performing Arts Venues

I can't promise there will always be theater performances at these venues, but they are known for hosting a variety of shows from Broadway and off-Broadway to regional theater shows seeking a larger venue. Check Web sites for schedules. Tickets can usually be purchased online or at the box office.

Adrienne Arsht Center for the Performing Arts

1300 Biscayne Blvd., Downtown Miami
(305) 949-6722
www.arshtcenter.org

American Airlines Arena

601 Biscayne Blvd., Downtown Miami
(786) 777-1000
www.aaarena.com
The Catch: Arena parking is no less than $15; there are lots in the neighborhood that may be cheaper, but you're better off carpooling and splitting the cost.

Bank of America Tower

100 SE 2nd St., Downtown Miami
(305) 539-7100
www.miamitower.net

Bayfront Park Amphitheater

301 North Biscayne Blvd., Downtown Miami
(305) 358-7550
www.bayfrontparkmiami.com

Colony Theater

1040 Lincoln Rd., Miami Beach
(305) 674-1040
www.colonytheaterfl.com

The Fillmore Miami Beach at the Jackie Gleason Theater
1700 Washington Ave., Miami Beach
(305) 673-7300
www.gleasontheater.com

James L. Knight Center
400 SE 2nd Ave., Downtown Miami
(305) 416-5970
www.jlkc.com

Lincoln Theatre
541 Lincoln Rd., Miami Beach
(305) 673-3330
www.nws.edu

The Lyric Theatre
819 NW 2nd Ave., Overtown
(305) 358-1146

Manuel Artime Theater
900 SW 1st St.
(305) 575-5057
www.manuelartimetheater.com

Miami Dade County Auditorium
2901 West Flagler St., Miami
(305) 547-5414
www.miamidade.gov

The Prometeo Theatre is part of Miami Dade College and showcases performances throughout the year. There is an emphasis on bilingualism so Spanish speakers, too, can enjoy what the theater has to offer. Call (305) 237-3262 or e-mail prometeo@mdc.edu for information on upcoming productions.

The Roxy Performing Arts Center
1645 SW 107th Ave., Westchester
(305) 226-0030
www.roxyperformingartscenter.com

The Roxy Theatre Group, affiliated with this facility, is geared toward children up to 17 years old. Performances are held year-round at their own venue and others around town. Tickets vary by performance. Call the box office for details.

Theatre Institute of South Florida
(305) 332-5817
www.thetheatreinstitute.com

The institute performs at various venues around the city and combines the talents of children and adult performers. Tickets are $12 in advance, when purchased on the Web site, and $20 at the door the day of the show. Shows are typically Fri and Sat at 8 p.m. and Sat and Sun at 2 p.m. Check the Web site for updated schedules. Venues are located at 3280 South Miami Ave., Miami Science Museum, Coconut Grove; 5300 NW 102nd Ave., Morgan Levy Park Community Center, Doral; and 5855 SW 111th St., Pinecrest Community Center, Pinecrest.

Unhinged Theatre
JCC Robert Russell Theater
11155 SW 112th Ave., Kendall
(305) 785-7377
www.unhingedtheatre.webs.com

Most shows are performed at the local JCC. Tickets are typically $15 for general adult admission and $10 for student admission. Call or e-mail unhinged theatre@gmail.com for more information.

PROFESSIONAL **THEATER**

Actors' Playhouse at The Miracle Theatre
280 Miracle Mile, Coral Gables
(305) 444-9293
www.actorsplayhouse.org

Ticket prices vary significantly based on the show. Some start at $15, others exceed $50. On Wed through Fri, tickets are always $15 for students 15 minutes before the show (subject to availability) courtesy of cultureshockmiami .com.

The Alliance Theatre Lab
15133 SW 142nd Court, SW Miami
(786) 276-1657
www.thealliancetheatrelab.com

Student and senior tickets start at $15 each and adult tickets are $20. Check the Web site for schedules and contact thealliancelab@aol.com for more information.

Ground Up and Rising, Inc.
Little Stage Theater
2100 Washington Ave., Miami Beach
(305) 529-6233
http://groundupandrising.org

The 2010 season included *Dying City* by Christopher Shinn, *The Pillowman* by Martin McDonagh, and *Violet Hour* by Richard Greenberg. Tickets are $15 for students, union members, and Miami Beach residents. Adult tickets are $25. Also take advantage of free Shakespeare in the Park, which happens yearly.

The Naked Stage
11300 NE 2nd Ave., Miami Shores
(954) 261-1785
www.nakedstage.org

This indie theater puts on classics like *Romeo and Juliet* but also is known for its 24 Hour Theatre event, Naked Stage, which showcases short plays that have been written and rehearsed in 24 hours. Tickets are $12 for students, $18 for seniors, and $25 for adults. Show times are Thurs through Sat at 8 p.m. and Sun at 2 p.m. and 7 p.m.

New Theatre
4120 Laguna St., Coral Gables
(305) 443-5909
www.new-theatre.org

Ticket prices start at $15 for student rush (excluding Shakespeare) half an hour before the show based on availability. Adult tickets may be as high as $40.

EVENTS:
FREE CELEBRATIONS

"Carnies built this country, the carnival part of it anyway. And though they may be rat-like in appearance, they are truly kings among men!"

—HOMER SIMPSON

A visitor would have to try very hard to come to Miami on a weekend where there wasn't a street fair, festival, carnival, or some kind of debauched event (usually with free drinks) happening. You'll find specific events (music, film, and specialty) in their respective sections, but there are a slew of festivals paying homage to books, families, culture, or, believe it or not, just staying up late. Check www.miamiandbeaches.com for frequent updates and new events.

STREET **FAIRS**, FESTIVALS, & CARNIVALS

Family Fun Fest
Biscayne National Park
9700 SW 328th St., Homestead
(305) 230-PARK (7275)

From December through April, this event is held the second Sun of every month. The program is free and includes hands-on activities that are themed around the environment and conservation.

Viernes Culturales (Cultural Fridays)
SW 8th St., Little Havana
(305) 643-5500
www.viernesculturales.org

Escape Miami Beach for a night and hit up the heart of Little Havana. The historically Cuban Calle Ocho neighborhood is never dull, but the last Fri of the month truly embodies the energy of Miami's Latin culture. Art exhibits, outdoor music, and local cuisine tasting are only a few of the fair's free offerings; neighborhood newbies can take gratis walking tours, too. Yes, Miami Beach's deco is part of local history, but the Little Havana neighborhood, including the 1926 Tower Theater, depicts Miami history inaccessible elsewhere. Plus, a trip to Miami is incomplete without legit Cuban food, and this is the place for it. The event takes place the last Fri of each month between 6:30 p.m. and 11 p.m. Contact info@viernesculturales.org for more information.

JANUARY

Art Deco Weekend Festival
Ocean Drive between 5th and 15th streets, Miami Beach
www.mdpl.org

Since 1976, the Miami Design and Preservation League has hosted this festival as an homage and awareness event to the arts and culture of the Art Deco era. Guided tours, lectures, a variety of vendors and performances, and parades will take place during the weekend on Miami Beach. This is the perfect opportunity to utilize the local shuttle, which costs 25 cents.

Beaux Arts Annual Festival of Arts
www.beauxartsmiami.org

This festival will celebrate its 60-year anniversary in January 2011. Admission is free all weekend to the festival itself, typically held at the University of Miami, and as an added art incentive, admission to the Lowe Art Museum is also free all weekend. Expect live music, delicious festival food, and lots o' art.

International Chocolate Festival
10901 Old Cutler Rd., Coral Gables
(305) 667-1651
www.fairchildgarden.org

This festival is unsurprisingly a hit, and has been held at Fairchild for the past several years. Lectures, cooking demonstrations, and tastings are offered, and the rest seems pretty self-explanatory. Admission ain't cheap, but you'll probably splurge if you really have a sweet tooth. It's $20 for adults, $15 for seniors, and $10 for children 6 to 17. Children five and under as well as Fairchild members are free.

Orange Bowl Fan Fest
Bayfront Park Amphitheater, Downtown Miami
www.orangebowl.org

If you're a die hard sports fan, this is the place to be the day before the big game. Typically held from 2 p.m. to 7 p.m., there's live music, games, and food. Best of all, you'll get to meet the players if you're lucky! Tickets typically cost $20 per person. Check the Web site for other affiliated events.

FEBRUARY

Caribbean Festival
Bayfront Park
301 North Biscayne Blvd., Downtown Miami
(305) 665-5379
www.bobmarleymovement.com

The Catch: Each attendee must bring four canned goods, which aren't expired!, in addition to the ticket for entrance.

This yearly event pays homage to the one and only Bob Marley with various well-known artists including Damien Marley, Shaggy, and other big reggae names. Gates are typically open from 1 p.m. to 11:30 p.m. the day of the event, rain or shine.

Coconut Grove Arts Festival
3390 Mary St., Coconut Grove
(305) 447-0401
www.coconutgroveartsfest.com

This festival is almost half a century old and typically attracts more than 10,000 people, which is no surprise given the 300+ international artists and craftsmen exhibiting. Festival food, live music, and Coconut Grove's atmosphere are additional incentives above the art itself. The typical weekend-long festival runs from 10 a.m. to 6 p.m. daily and costs $10 per person. Children 12 and under as well as Metrorail Golden Passport and Patriot Passport holders are free. Coconut Grove residents get half off admission with ID.

Miami Beach Antique Show
Miami Beach Convention Center
1901 Convention Center Dr., Miami Beach
(239) 732-6642
www.originalmiamibeachantiqueshow.com

A $15 pass is valid for all five days of this yearly show, which attracts antique sellers from all over the place. Hours typically run from noon to 8 p.m. most days of the festival.

Miami International Boat Show and Strictly Sail

Miami Beach Convention Center
1901 Convention Center Dr., Miami Beach
www.miamiboatshow.com

Typically held at the Miami Beach Convention Center, this is a perfect place to go if you want to see pretty things but not buy them. My favorite thing to do is tour the giant yachts. (If you're ballsy enough, dress nicely to fake sellers out!) Admission starts at $16 for adults but is free for children 12 and under.

Saint Sophia Greek Festival

Saint Sophia Greek Orthodox Cathedral
2401 SW 3rd Ave., Miami
(305) 854-2922
www.saintsophiagreekfestival.com

Their economy isn't looking so great, but their food and wine still are. One weekend in February from 11 a.m. to 11 p.m. each day, gorge yourself on Greek grub and cultural activities. The entry fee is only $5 (and $2 off with the ad on the Web site) but there's typically free admission on the first day of the fest before 5 p.m. Children under 12 get in free.

South Miami Rotary Art Festival

5750 SW 72nd St., South Miami
www.southmiamiartfest.org

For almost 30 years this festival has run for a full weekend at the end of February, typically from 10 a.m. to 6 p.m. Entrance is typically free, but finding parking is the tricky part.

VolleyPalooza

Ocean Drive and 8th St., Miami Beach
www.southbeachvolleyball.com

Don't be fooled: the only cause being supported here is a drooling audience watching local Miami models jump around in bikinis. The sport is taken seriously and breeds some good competition among models represented at local agencies, including Wilhelmina, Ford, and other big names.

MARCH

Dade Heritage Days
www.dadeheritagetrust.org

The Catch: There are some legitimately free events, but a handful are not, so check prices before you commit.

From the beginning of March to the end of April, the Dade Heritage Trust celebrates the history of the city with free and cheap events throughout the city. This includes free tours, entrance to parks, and fairs.

Miami International Agriculture and Cattle Show
Tropical Park
7900 SW 40th St., Miami
(305) 228-3414
www.miacs.info

Miami never fails to shock you; who'da thunk a cattle show would fit nicely in between the months of models playing beach volleyball and the gay pride parade overtaking South Beach?

APRIL

Art in the Park
Ponce Circle Park
2800 Ponce de Leon Blvd., Coral Gables
(305) 644-8888
www.carnavalmiami.com/artintheparkconcerts

This concert series typically happens right after Tax Day with a final bash featuring two-for-one drink specials, live music, and other free and fun exhibits.

Gay Pride
www.miamibeachgaypride.com

Every April, the local Gay Pride festival happens on Ocean Drive from 5th to 15th Streets. The festival typically takes place from noon to 8 p.m. at Lummus Park between 10th and 14th streets and features an expo of more than 100 varied vendors, live music, and a stage.

Miami Goin' Green Earth Day Festival

Bayfront Park
301 North Biscayne Blvd., Downtown Miami
www.miamigoingreen.com

I bet you can guess when this yearly festival takes place. Best of all, entrance to the event is free and it typically runs from 10 a.m. to 6 p.m. There are demonstrations and performances galore and food and drinks are available for purchase.

Miami Riverday Commission

Lummus Park Historic District
250 NW North River Dr., Miami
(305) 644-0544
www.miamirivercommission.org

Every May this event features live music, riverboat rides, and other river-related activities. The festival is always free.

Sunfest Music Festival

Florida's Intracoastal Waterway
(800) SUNFEST (786-3378)
www.sunfest.com

This fest is a bit further north in West Palm Beach, but the tri-rail goes there and the lineup is typically spectacular. Past years have included Weezer, Ben Harper, Patti Labelle, The Flaming Lips, and various other big names. The event typically includes a craft show, youth park, and fireworks show the last night of the festival. One-day passes start at $30, which isn't bad considering the quality of the acts you get to see. Kids 5 and under are free and one-day passes for kids 6 to 12 are $8.

MAY

Aqua Girl

www.aquagirl.org

The Catch: Many events are cheaper with pre-purchase, so buy your tickets early if possible. Also, most events are 21 and over only, though a few allow 18-and-overs.

They coin this "A week-long celebration for women who love women," so prepare for a serious party. It's technically a fundraiser so some events do carry a price tag (i.e. the opening night VIP cocktail reception for $95 at the door) but other events are reasonable and sort of a deal; the Lady Luck Bowlathon is only $15 for entrance and two games. When have you ever bowled for that cheap? Check the Web site for schedules and details.

Redland International Orchid Show
Fruit and Spice Park
24801 SW 187th Ave., Homestead
www.redlandorchidfestival.org

Every May this weekend festival attracts orchid lovers from all over. The $7 admission sounds steep but the event also offers walking tours of the park by orchidists, supplies, lectures and demonstrations, crafts, and a variety of food and drink available for purchase.

Rib and Beer Fest
Fritz & Franz Bierhaus
60 Merrick Way, Coral Gables
(305) 774-1883
www.bierhaus.cc

Live entertainment and the obvious will overwhelm this yearly festival, typically held over a weekend in late May. Take advantage of a hefty beer selection and unique rib flavors. Opening hours are usually 8 p.m. to midnight Fri and Sat and 5 to 9 p.m. on Sun.

Swap Miami
297 NW 23rd Street at Cafeina, Miami
www.swapmiami.com

Any real cheap bastard will not miss this opportunity. Instead of donating your stuff to Goodwill, donate it to other cheap bastards and sort through their stuff for hidden treasures. The swap includes clothing and home items, including furniture. Tickets are $8 in advance online or $10 at the door.

JUNE

Goombay Festival
www.goombayfestivalcoconutgrove.com

For over 30 years every June, this colorful event has attracted all walks of life for dancing, drinking, and general debauchery. The street festival is typically on Sun from noon to 8 p.m. and is deemed "the world's largest 'stepping' party." Don't miss that or the Sun morning gospel service, typically from 11 a.m. to 1 p.m., if you're a fan.

Redland Summer Fruit Festival
Fruit and Spice Park
24801 SW 187th Ave., Homestead
www.fruitandspicepark.org

If you're looking for something a little different than your average apple, swing by this festival, which costs $8 for adults and is free for children 10 and under. Rare fruit samplings are available to try (and buy!) and other wines and foods are also available for purchase.

JULY

Mercedes-Benz Fashion Week
www.mbfashionweek.com

The Catch: Unless you're a celeb or member of the media, scoring a volunteer position will be your best bet to get in the door.

If you've seen *The Devil Wears Prada* you probably know that Fashion Week is a pretty exclusive happening and typically requires tickets for all events. But the event does accept volunteers, which yields some opportunity to see shows and attend parties. E-mail MBFWVolunteers@imgworld.com and do not call, as the Web site warns against it.

The Summer Groove
www.thesummergroove.com

Hosted by Alonzo Mourning and Dwyane Wade, this yearly event features a free block party and various (paid) events that donate all proceeds to the athletes' charities. The Block Party is what you don't want to miss; there's typically free grub, and celeb spotting isn't unusual.

OCTOBER

Columbus Day Regatta

While Americans in the Northeast are freezing in the midst of winter, bask in the sun and admire (lots and lots) of skin during this day-long festival. You'll need a boat to get the full effect of this event, at which you can expect to witness plenty of wildness. The boats swarm each other in Biscayne Bay, mainly, but also crowd in other spots around the city. The regatta usually lasts all day Sat and Sun over Columbus Day weekend.

Miami Attractions Month

www.amazingmiamiattractions.com

Highlighting—you guessed it!—Miami's attractions, this month-long festival will yield some serious free and cheap deals around the city. Check the Web site for specials and details.

Miami Beach Antique Jewelry and Watch Show

Miami Beach Convention Center
1901 Convention Center Dr., Miami Beach
www.miamibeachantiquejewelryandwatchshow.com

This is not a typo or repeat of the above antique show; in fact, according to the Web site, this is the largest show of its kind and features international exhibitors. Show hours are typically 11 a.m. to 7 p.m. on Fri and Sat and until 6 p.m. on Sun. Admission is $15 per person for all three days of the show.

Miami Carnival

Bicentennial Park
301 North Biscayne Blvd., Downtown Miami
http://miamicarnival.net

Running for the past 25 years, this is the closest you'll get to the authentic, celebratory carnival in Brazil. Expect dancing, eating, and music, as well as lots o' Brazilian flavor and skin.

Oktoberfest

Fritz & Franz Bierhaus
60 Merrick Way, Coral Gables
(305) 774-1883
www.bierhaus.cc

Can't make it to Germany for the ultimate beer-lovers festival? Stop by this local Oktoberfest for drink specials and German pride.

NOVEMBER

Harvest Festival

Miami Dade Fair Expo
10901 Coral Way, Sweetwater/Kendall area
(386) 860-0092
www.miamiharvest.webs.com

This is your chance to buy a perfect pumpkin and pretend that there are seasons in the city despite the 90-degree weather. General admission is $8 per person for adults, $2 for children from 5 to 12 years old, and free for children under 4. The Web site lists a $2 coupon for adult admission only and is limited to two per family.

Miami Book Fair International

Downtown Miami
www.miamibookfair.com

Dozens of authors flock to Miami to promote their new releases, but the real treat is the free street fair that begins the Fri of the festival.

Sleepless Night

Miami Beach
(305) 673-7577
www.sleeplessnight.org

Sleepless Night is the ultimate cheap bastard's paradise; all over Miami Beach one night a year (usually in November) businesses throughout the beach open their doors all night and offer free . . . everything! Movie screenings, food, drinks, entertainment, you name it! Free shuttle buses are provided to and from various events and a detailed schedule of events is released before the events.

White Party Week

www.whiteparty.org

It sounds like a P. Diddy extravaganza, but this event is specifically dedicated to HIV/AIDS and touts itself as the world's oldest and largest fundraiser for the cause.

DECEMBER

Art Basel

Miami Beach
(305) 674-1292
www.artbaselmiamibeach.com

This yearly event isn't cheap, but free showings at galleries are typically included in the schedule. The festival also hosts multiple music performances that take place throughout the event, many of which are free.

FOOD & DRINK:
PAY FOR IT TOMORROW
MORNING

"Once, during Prohibition, I was forced to live for days on nothing but food and water."

—AMERICAN COMEDIAN W. C. FIELDS

Even in snazzy, swanky see-and-be-seen Miami, spendthrifts can hang out and eat out undetected. What's more, with the depth of culture in the city, fusion cuisines are boundless and you'll never be at a loss for dining options. There are the classy restaurants (i.e. Barton G or Nobu) but there are also more homey, cultural, and down to earth options that I'd recommend even if you do have money to splurge.

Wander through high-end supermarkets and specialty stores around the city and you will find a delightful (and filling) selection of samples to chow down on. Make your way to a number of bars and restaurants that offer impressive drink and food specials during happy hour, or hit venues on discount days or during early-bird specials, and you'll have plenty of cash left at the end of the day.

If you are female, you're in luck—oodles of establishments offer ladies night specials with open bars for several hours. It's not unheard of for bars to have open bars for both sexes, too. It is tough to choose with so many deals, but most of the work is done for you. Flip further and you'll know where to go and when for the best deals in town.

ALL-**YOU**-CAN-**EAT** & **BUFFETS**

I'm not saying these are classy or swanky joints; I am saying you can get a bang for your buck and that is likely why you are reading this book. Some all-you-can-eat joints are pricey, but there are a few options in Miami that have decent deals. Just beware: some restaurants have specific rules and regulations about sharing, leaving food, and taking home leftovers for these types of deals. So order wisely and go hungry!

Bellante's Pizza and Pasta
8734 Mills Dr., Kendall
(305) 598-6800

For $5.93, you cannot beat this all-you-can-eat special that includes a buffet of pizza, pasta, and salad. They're open daily from 11 a.m. to 10 p.m. and children can enjoy the same deal for $3 each.

Boteco

916 NE 79th St., NE Miami
(305) 757-7735
www.botecomiami.com

This Brazilian joint has all-you-can-eat specials throughout the week. Recently these have included all-you-can-eat skewers (filet, shrimp, chicken, sausage) for $12.99 from 6 to 11 p.m. on Tues and all-you-can-eat appetizers for $9.50 on Wed.

Dynasty Buffet

1656 NE Miami Gardens Dr., Miami Gardens
(305) 919-7705

This giant Chinese buffet is a steal any day or time throughout the week. Prices start at $6.75 for adult buffets during the week and $7.75 on Sat and Sun. Dinner prices are $9.95 during the week and $11.55 on Sat and Sun. The buffet is open from 11:30 a.m. to 10 p.m. daily and year-round. Discounts apply for children and they eat completely free if they are under three years old.

Kebab Indian Restaurant

514 NE 167th St., North Miami
(305) 940-6309
http://kebabindia.com

Of all the cultural food available in the city, Indian is not one that you'll find all over the place. (Cuban, on the other hand . . .) So take advantage of this $10.99 all-you-can-eat lunch special from 11:30 a.m. to 3 p.m. The restaurant is closed on Mon.

The Knife

3444 Grand Ave., Coconut Grove
(786) 866-3999
www.thekniferestaurant.com

Any true carnivore should make a trip to this place, which has all-you-can-eat specials with unlimited amounts of meat. They credit themselves with being unique for including the drink and dessert in the final price—though I'm not sure how it is humanly possible to eat dessert after consuming this much food. Meat choices include beef, filet, and various cuts of steak and chicken. Mon to Fri, lunch costs $20.95; it's $25.95 on the weekends. Take advantage of the special Mon to Fri lunch, which is $16.95 and includes a glass of wine. Dinner starts at $26.75 and is $29.65 on weekend nights. Sun through Thurs they are open from 11:30 a.m. to 11 p.m. and 11:30 a.m. to midnight on Fri and Sat.

La Palma Ristorante
116 Alhambra Circle, Coral Gables
(305) 445-8777
www.lapalmaristorante.com

The Catch: Dessert not included.

This fancy joint opens its doors to cheapskates Mon through Fri from 11:30 a.m. to 3 p.m. with their famous lunch buffet for $12.95. The menu is constantly changing so even if you make a weekly visit, you will not get bored. Typically the buffet includes salads, soups, and pastas.

Miyako Restaurant
18090 Collins Ave., Sunny Isles Beach
(305) 931-0455

You can't beat this all you can eat sushi deal for $13.95 anytime. They are open Mon through Thurs from 11:30 a.m. to 11 p.m., Fri and Sat from 11:30 a.m. to 11:30 p.m., and Sun from noon to 11 p.m.

Out of the Blue Café and Wine Bar
2426 NE 2nd Ave., Downtown Miami
(305) 573-3800
www.outofthebluecafe.net

This $19.95 Sun brunch is an all-you-can-eat deal that runs from 10 a.m. to 5 p.m. weekly. A mimosa is included in brunch; there is also free Wi-Fi.

Prana Health Food and Vegetarian Restaurant
7293 NW 36th St., Doral
(305) 594-6966

Take advantage of this healthy $9 all-you-can-eat buffet from 11 a.m. to 4 p.m. every day except Sun.

Cooking Classes

Chef Allen's Modern Seafood Bistro

19088 NE 29th Ave., Aventura

(305) 935-2900

www.chefallens.com

The Catch: It's only offered at certain times of the year and is limited to 50 participants, which are selected on a first come, first served basis.

This chef offers free cooking classes on Fri from 6 to 7 p.m. for 50 lucky participants. There is free parking and the class includes wine and menu samples.

Macy's Cooking School

Dadeland Kids and Home Store

7675 North Kendall Dr., Kendall

(305) 662-3550

Every Sat at 1 p.m. there are free cooking classes. A second location is at The Cellar Aventura in the Men and Home Store at Aventura Mall, 19535 Biscayne Blvd. (305-577-2296).

Whole Foods Market Coral Gables

6701 Red Rd., Coral Gables

(305) 421-9421

The Catch: Make reservations to pre-register beforehand by calling the listed number.

This establishment offers free cooking classes and demonstrations throughout the month. Check the Web site or call for details.

Shinju Japanese Buffet
8800 SW 72nd St., Kendall

(305) 275-8801

This $10 all-you-can-eat lunch buffet is a steal.

Tokyo Bowl
12290 Biscayne Blvd., North Miami
(305) 892-9400

If you're a sushi fanatic and love tempura, you'll soon be a fixture at Tokyo Bowl's $14 all-you-can-eat deal.

BACK **TO** BASICS

There are restaurants in the city that are just plain good. They don't have any standout atmosphere (except for people-watching, perhaps), but they do have delicious grub, and that is what keeps their clientele coming back.

8 oz. Burger Bar
1080 Alton Rd., Miami Beach
(305) 397-8246

Voted one of the best burgers in Miami, this spot uses the best quality beef and has $5 drink specials all the time. They are open Sun through Wed from 11 a.m. to midnight and Thurs through Sat from 11 a.m. to 2 a.m.

Casola's
2437 SW 17th Ave., Coral Gables
(305) 858-0090

The Catch: It's a cash-only joint, so come prepared.

This local pizzeria is, unsurprisingly, known for its delicious pizza at $3.77 per slice. But try the wings, too!

El Pub Restaurant
1548 SW 8th St., Little Havana
(305) 642-9942

"Basic is better" should be the tagline at this Latin favorite. Daily specials are listed on the Web site and you can't beat entrees plus two sides that run about $6. You can't go wrong with anything on the menu, but if you're an adventurous eater, try the Beef Brain Fritters or the Pig's Feet Creole.

El Rey de las Fritas

1677 SW 107th Ave., Sweetwater area
(305) 223-7260
http://reydelasfritas.com

This place is in a strip mall so you're not going for the scenery. You are going for the original Cuban frita, a Cuban hamburger with onion and shoestring potatoes. The original will only set you back $3 and even the "fancier" dishes aren't much more. Two additional locations are at 421 West 29th St., Hialeah (305-863-0880) and 1821 SW 8th St., Little Havana (305-644-6054).

Five Guys

Dadeland Plaza
9457 South Dixie Hwy., Pinecrest
(305) 669-2115
www.fiveguys.com

Okay, it is a chain, but it's also a local favorite and preferable to any world-wide fast food joint that's been featured in documentaries about the fast food industry. Traditional burgers and fries are their specialties. Two other locations are at Kendall Village, 10471 SW 88th St., Suite B-10, Kendall (305-270-4990) and 1540 South Dixie Hwy., Coral Gables (305-740-5972).

Half Moon Empanadas

1616 Washington Ave., Miami Beach
(305) 532-5277
www.halfmoonempanadas.com

Their combos are a sweet deal, including $5.99 for two empanadas and a drink or coffee. Or, order their many flavors of empanadas individually, which are $2.19 each. A second location is at 192 SE 1st Ave., Downtown Miami (305-379-2525).

Here Comes the Sun

2188 NE 123rd St., North Miami
(305) 893-5711

This Miami health joint is a must for vegans, vegetarians, or general health nuts. Do not leave without trying the sun sauce! My personal favorite is the $5.95 brown rice and soy cheese dish that could feed a small army.

Jerry's Deli

1450 Collins Ave., Miami Beach
(305) 532-8030
www.jerrysfamousdeli.com

Admittedly, it is a chain. But it's included here with good reason. The grub is standard deli food, but with more than 600 items on the menu, it's impossible not to find something you like. Plus, it's a great place to go with kids and for an atmosphere that attracts some great local characters.

La Palma Restaurant

6091 SW 8th St., Little Havana
(305) 261-1113

This is another hole-in-the-wall, which is so worth it if you're looking for local Latin food. Their no-frill croquetas are 86 cents each and rated the best in the city by the *Miami New Times*. It wouldn't hurt to know a few words in Spanish before ordering.

La Sandwicherie

229 14th St., Miami Beach
(305) 532-8934
www.lasandwicherie.com

This is a hidden local favorite with solid sandwiches and a juice bar. The location and hours are also ideal for late night snacking; they are open daily from 8 a.m. to 5 a.m. and Fri and Sat until 6 a.m. Delivery is limited to the hours of 11 a.m. and 10 p.m. daily, but you can always go into the restaurant for a midnight snack!

Mama Jennie's Italian Restaurant

11720 NE 2nd Ave., Miami
(305) 757-3627
www.mamajennies.com

Finding a decent Italian restaurant anywhere in the world may be a simple task, but finding one that's reasonably priced and unpretentious isn't always as easy. Mama Jennie's has been around for more than 35 years and even with its rock bottom prices still offers coupons on the Web site. Mon through Fri lunch specials are only $5.95. Dinner pastas start around $7.95 and include unlimited garlic rolls and soup or salad.

Miyako Japanese Restaurant
9533 South Dixie Hwy., Kendall
(305) 668-9367

This isn't the absolute cheapest, but it is a personal local favorite that is always affordable and delicious. An additional location is at 5844 SW 73rd St., South Miami (305-663-7166).

Papo Llega y Pon
2928 NW 17th Ave., Miami
(305) 635-0137

The $5 pork sandwich is a must—some say the best in town. It's not a flashy joint, so keep your eyes peeled on NW 17th Avenue between 29th and 30th Streets.

Paquito's Mexican Restaurant
16265 Biscayne Blvd., Sunny Isles Beach
(305) 947-5027
http://paquitosmiami.com

Giant stuffed 10-inch burritos start at $10, but you can also order "North of the border" foods including hamburgers and the like.

Plate
2135 Coral Way, Brickell
(305) 854-1888
http://plateinmiami.com

This adorable lunch joint offers just the right balance of variety and portion control. The menu changes daily, so never worry about getting bored. Weekly specials are posted online and cost $7.50 for one daily grouping of plates. These dishes range from turkey picadillo, black beans, and brown rice to fish or chicken breast in marinara sauce, tri-color tortellini, and salad. Also take advantage of the one-week plan for $38 per week.

Rice House of Kebab
1318 Alton Rd., Miami Beach
(305) 531-0332
www.ricehouseofkabob.com

Whole Foods, Half Price

For other basics for your home, Whole Foods is a good place to start. Despite its nickname, "Whole Paycheck," there are items (and the occasional free sample!) for which bargain shoppers should keep an eye out. Their 365 store brand is typically inexpensive and the store often hosts many free and cheap classes and events. Days vary, but many are held on Tues, Wed, and Fri. Check the individual store Web sites for details.

Classes and events range from wine lounge nights with free tastings to healthy bodies workshops teaching you how to eat healthy on a budget (err, by shopping elsewhere, right?) and gluten-free food tastings. Non-food events like wellness fairs with complimentary, five-minute chair massages and baby-wearing meet-ups teaching moms various ways to carry their infants in a sling are regularly on offer, too. This is also a great store to wander through, if only for the free samples.

21105 Biscayne Blvd., Aventura
(305) 933-1543
www.wholefoodsmarket.com/stores/aventura

6701 Red Rd., Coral Gables
(305) 421-9421
www.wholefoodsmarket.com/stores/coralgables

1020 Alton Rd., Miami Beach
(305) 532-1707
www.wholefoodsmarket.com/stores/southbeach

11701 South Dixie Hwy., Pinecrest
(305) 971-0900
www.wholefoodsmarket.com/stores/pinecrest

The atmosphere is cute, but nothing to write home about. The rice on the other hand . . . Everything on this menu is delicious, especially (surprise!) the rice dishes. For a new flavor, try the Zereshk Polo, which is basmati rice drizzled with a sweet and sour barberry-cinnamon reduction. The Adas Polo, lentils and raisins in basmati rice, is also delicious. Two additional locations are at 1450 NW 87th Ave., Doral (305-418-9464); and 13742 SW 56th St., Kendall (305-387-6815).

Samurai
8717 SW 136th St., Kendall
(305) 238-2131
www.benihana.com

You've never been to a teppanyaki restaurant until you've been to Samurai. It's a sister brand to Benihana . . . but so much better. From noon to 3:30 p.m. Mon through Fri, their lunch specials start at $9.

INTERNATIONAL & ECLECTIC FLAVOR

Big Pink
157 Collins Ave., Miami Beach
(305) 532-4700
www.mylesrestaurantgroup.com

This is a Miami staple, which you should either visit at 4 a.m. after a night of dancing at Opium nightclub across the street, for brunch, or both. Everything on the menu is delicious, but I particularly recommend the sweet potato fries. Take advantage of free delivery from 9 a.m. to midnight (and 1 a.m. on Fri and Sat). Pink is owned by a big name company and the portion sizes reflect their ego.

Café Pastis
7310 Red Rd., South Miami
(305) 665-3322
www.cafepastis.com

This South Miami gem is a slice of France. The French onion soup is among the best, and other traditional dishes (and desserts!) are to die for.

Charlotte Bakery
1499 Washington Ave., Miami Beach
(305) 535-0095
www.charlottebakeryinc.com

The owner, a Chile native, does not discriminate when it comes to empanadas; the bakery is known for its Chilean, Argentine, and Venezuelan flavors, which is not surprising considering she lived in two of the three countries. Empanadas cost around $3 each, and Argentine flavors can be as cheap as $1.75. They also sell Latin American candy and have catering services.

David's Café
1058 Collins Ave., Miami Beach
(305) 534-8736
http://davidscafe.com

This 24/7 spot is one of the beach's best known for serious coffee and breakfast grub. Opened by Cuban immigrants in 1977, it's impossible to leave hungry with their hefty portions and choices of breakfast, dinner, and anytime lunch menu. A second Miami Beach location is at 1654 Meridian Ave. (305-672-8707).

Dogma Grill
7030 Biscayne Blvd., North Miami
(305) 759-3433
www.dogmagrill.com

This might take the cake as the home of all cheap bastards in Miami: a $3.15 dog. You can also get a hot dog that's fancy enough to be $5.95, some topped with cucumbers and tomatoes to various types of cheeses. Salads and vegetarian sides are also available. They're open Mon through Sun 10 a.m. through 9 p.m.

Hot Dog Hankering

If you want a good ol' dog but don't want to wait until baseball season, here are a couple other joints that'll satisfy your craving and save your wallet.

Arbetter Hot Dogs
8747 SW 40th St., SW Miami
(305) 207-0555
Standard dogs and chili fries, but a favorite among locals.

Los Perros
8410 West Flagler St., West Miami
(786) 953-6845
www.losperros.com
Dogs are the specialty, but burgers, arepas, and Latin favorites are also on the menu.

El Nuevo Siglo
1305 SW 8th St., Little Havana
(305) 854-1916

It has a reputation for having some of the best Cuban food in this part of town, which is no small feat. Hours are daily from 7 a.m. to 7 p.m.

Europa Car Wash and Café
6075 Biscayne Blvd., Little Haiti
(305) 751-9681

Talk about multi-tasking! This is the place to go for a local flavor plus efficiency. There is outdoor seating and free Wi-Fi, so it's a great place to work, people-watch, and leave with a clean car. Hours are 6 a.m. to 10 p.m. daily.

Hofbräu Beerhall Miami
943 Lincoln Rd., Miami Beach
(305) 538-8066
www.hofbraumiami.com

If you can't afford a flight to Germany, this is the closest you'll get in Miami. Expect your German favorites including Hofbräu Gulaschsuppe (goulash soup), Kartoffelpfannkuchen (potato pancakes) and several variations of Wiener Schnitzel. It's not the cheapest food (potato pancakes are $8) but there is a beer happy hour on Wed, which makes the pricier food worth the trip.

Hy Vong
3458 SW 8th St., Little Havana
(305) 446-3674
www.hyvong.com

It's a local Vietnamese favorite that is also reasonably priced. Try specialties including roasted lamb chops with spicy mango chutney, barbecued pork with vermicelli rice noodles, or fish wrapped in pastry with watercress cream cheese dressing, among other unique dishes.

Jaguar Ceviche Spoon Bar and Grill
3067 Grand Ave., Coconut Grove
(305) 444-0216
www.jaguarspot.com

Outdoor seating is ample, but you can also sit at the traditional or ceviche bar if you're having a hankering for a drink or something raw. The highlight of this spot is the spoon bar, which allows you a taste of a variety of dishes for only $2 each. Try the $12 sampler or order a full portion of any dish starting at $12. There are plenty of other dishes as well as an $11 lunch special from 11:30 a.m. to 3:30 p.m. Mon through Fri except holidays.

Jimmy's Eastside Diner
7201 Biscayne Blvd., NE Miami
(305) 751-8882

It's a perfect place to nurse a hangover with all the essentials: eggs, pancakes, and coffee. Everything is cheap and the service is reliable.

Joe's Stone Crab
11 Washington Ave., Miami Beach
(305) 673-0365
www.joesstonecrab.com

The Catch: Takeout sides are cheap. Stone crabs are not.

The sides alone are worth a trip there. Consider ordering takeout for a picnic. The moment you start ordering seafood it'll get pricey, but the sides are delicious and not outrageously priced. Favorites include hashed browns for $6.25, creamed spinach for $5.25 and Joe's Famous Key Lime Pie for $6.95.

La Carreta
3632 SW 8th St., Little Havana
(305) 444-7501
www.lacarreta.com

Skip the airport version of this lauded Miami restaurant, and instead try one of their other many locations. Atmosphere is an important component of this experience—though I would argue that eating plantains is equally weighty. Daily specials are always on the menu and the grub is pretty cheap. Additional locations are at 10633 NW 12th St., Doral (305-463-9778); 11740 SW 88th St., Kendall (305-596-5973); and 8650 Bird Rd., West Miami (305-553-8383).

La Parilla Liberty
609 Washington Ave., Miami Beach
(305) 532-7599

This joint is a fusion of Argentine and Italian flavors. Try the empanadas for only $1.50 or the $12 pasta that ranges from ravioli to fettuccine.

Lime Fresh Mexican Grill
3201 North Miami Ave. Suite 100, Miami
(305) 576-5463
www.limefreshmexicangrill.com

This yummy Mexican place has everything you would expect a Mexican joint to have, but better. Most locations are open daily from 11 a.m. to 10 p.m. Check the Web site for additional locations in the area.

Lost and Found Saloon
185 NW 36th St., Downtown Miami
(305) 576-1008
www.thelostandfoundsaloon-miami.com

This slice of the West in the South is a local restaurant with character. Open at 11 a.m. every day and until 10 p.m. Sun through Thurs and midnight Fri and Sat, the menu has a decent barbecue selection in addition to a giant selection of brews and wines.

Macitas Restaurant and Bakery

18503 South Dixie Hwy., Palmetto Bay
(305) 259-0404
www.macitas.com

When was the last time you ate an omelet for $3.75? This Latin spot has all the basics, including super duper cheap favorites including croquetas and empanadas.

Monty's Stone Crab and Seafood

2550 South Bayshore Dr., Coconut Grove
(305) 856-3992
http://montysbayshore.com

On 365 days per year this joint has stone crabs from somewhere! Take advantage of half-off stone crabs during happy hour. The Florida season runs from mid-October through mid-May and Monty's serves other claws for the rest of the year. This is also a great spot to go for late-night outdoor dancing, which happens almost any night at various locations. Another Monty's is located at 300 Alton Rd., Miami Beach (305-672-1148, www.montyssouthbeach.com).

Palace Bar and Restaurant
1200 Ocean Dr., Miami Beach
(305) 531-7234
www.palacesouthbeach.com

If the drag show itself wasn't enough, enjoy their leisurely "Sunday Brunchic" at 11:30 a.m. or 2 p.m., which includes brunch, mimosas, and limitless entertainment for $29.99 per person.

Soyka's Restaurant, Café and Bar
5582 NE 4th Court, Downtown Miami
(305) 759-3117

This restaurant was a pioneer of the Downtown neighborhood. Always good food, the menu typically features standard American fare and an impressive list of wines and after dinner drinks. Soyka is open from 11 a.m. to 11 p.m. Sun through Thurs and until midnight on Fri and Sat.

Taverna Opa
36–40 Ocean Dr., Miami Beach
(305) 673-6730
www.tavernaoparestaurant.com

Consider this an alternative dining experience—the highlight being encouragement to dance on tables that are covered with food. This Greek-style tavern will have you dance enough that whatever you eat will be burned off by the end of the night. A Fort Lauderdale location is at 3051 NE 32nd Ave. (954-567-1630).

Versailles
3555 SW 8th St., Little Havana
(305) 444-0240
www.versaillescuban.com

Yet another Cuban restaurant, and oh so worth it. Everything is delicious and best of all, cheap. Chicken dishes start as low as $6.50. And don't even bother going if you're not going to order platanos and/or maduros.

SWEET **TOOTH**

2 Girls and a Cupcake
140 SE 1st Ave., Miami
(305) 373-8001
www.2cupcakegirls.com

Try Java Junkie (chocolate cupcake with espresso butter cream) or Rice
Krispy Cup (vanilla cupcake with rice krispy baked in and topped with
marshmallow vanilla butter cream) among other unique flavors. Sizes range
from $1 minis to $2.99 jumbos.

Buttercream Cupcakes and Coffee
1411 Sunset Dr., Coral Gables
(305) 669-8181
www.buttercreamcupcakes.com

At least eight flavors are offered daily, so check the Web site for details on
what flavors are available when. The usual chocolate, vanilla, and red velvet
are on the menu, but also look out for latte, lime, and Oreo flavors. Individual cupcakes can be purchased for $2.75 and a baker's dozen is $33 and
can be ordered on the Web site.

Delices de France
14453 South Dixie Hwy., Palmetto Bay
(305) 256-9700

Baguettes. Croissants. You name it. This place was named Best Bakery and
with mini baguettes starting at 50 cents and most other pastries under $3
it's a well-deserved title.

Gelateria Parmalat
670 Lincoln Rd., Miami Beach
(786) 276-9475

Skip all the average Lincoln Road gelato joints and hit up Parmalat for the
same couple bucks. You may remember this milk brand as a child, but the
gelato is a whole separate animal. Flavors vary daily but it's always fun to
sample the milk flavor and evoke childhood memories.

The Cupcake Diva

Danielle Glirten *is* the cupcake diva. It's basically impossible not to find a flavor you like among the dozens. And if you can't, she will. A few highlights: The Little Miss Priss, a vanilla cake made with bourbon Madagascar vanilla bean, infused with a Kahlua center and topped with a vanilla bean cream cheese frosting. Another: Old Key West, a key lime sponge cake made with the freshest key lime juice and topped off with a delicious cream cheese frosting.

Those are only two mouthwatering examples. At the moment, you can buy her cupcakes at **Broadway Bagels** at 13854 SW 88th Street in Kendall, reachable at (305) 385-0790. Mini cupcakes are $1 each and regular sized cupcakes are $2.50 each. Want them to match your invitation or sports celebration? She'll customize anything for minimal extra charges. Vegans should keep an eye out for potential vegan recipe developments. There is no minimum order. Contact Danielle at (305) 968-5512 or danielle@thecupcakedivamiami.com. Check the Web site, www.cupcakedivamiami.com, for a full flavor list and photos.

LA Sweets

The Shops at Sunset Place
5701 Sunset Dr., South Miami
(305) 665-5288
www.lasweets.net

Mango, pumpkin, sweet potato cupcake? These and other unique flavors are among the hundreds you can choose from, which can be purchased individually starting at $1.25 each. Buy four or more and get a price reduction to $1 each.

Misha's Cupcakes

1548 South Dixie Hwy., Coral Gables
(786) 200-6153
www.mishascupcakes.com

Expect a burst of creativity from this new store, which creates cakes made out of cupcakes in customizable shapes and designs. Individual cupcakes start at $1.25 and 6-inch cakes are $20.

Sweetness Bake Shop and Café
9549 Sunset Dr., South Miami
(305) 271-7791
www.sweetnessbakeshop.net

Two specials you should know about: free cupcake on your birthday and for kids 12 and under with straight A's on their report card. Another sinful spot with every imaginable flavor, cupcakes are $1 for mini, $2 for regular and $3 for jumbo. Gelato, cakes, and other sweets are available.

Wall's Old Fashioned Ice Cream
8075 Ludlam Road, South Miami
(305) 740-9830

This is a Miami classic with every imaginable old school menu item in the book: ice cream floats, sodas, milk shakes, and malts.

Whip 'N Dip Ice Cream
1407 Sunset Dr., South Miami
(305) 665-2565
www.whipndipicecream.com

Don't go right after school or you'll run into a swarm of hungry children, but any other time enjoy this local favorite, which has been around since the mid-1980s.

Versailles Bakery
3501 SW 8th St., Little Havana
(305) 441-2500

This is your go-to Cuban bakery in Miami, which is reliably delicious and reasonably priced. Empanadas, pastelitos, and croquettes are crowd favorites.

Via Veneto Gelateria
13770 SW 84th St., Kendall
(305) 752-0833
http://viavenetogelateria.com

You'll find every imaginable gelato flavor, including interesting dulce de leche, tiramisu, and zabaione.

Yiya's on 79th Street
646 NE 79th St., NE Miami
(305) 754-3337
www.yiyas.com

The food is good, but the baked goods are to die for. Try the Cuban bread, including a whole fresh loaf or a Cuban toast with butter for $1.25. Desserts range from filled croissants for 95 cents to homemade brownies and cake slices for $2. If you really want to fit in, try the $3 traditional Cuban flan.

FARMERS' MARKETS & FRUIT STANDS

If you have a weakness for farmers' markets and the like, first check www .themarketcompany.org for weekly market schedules. Below are a few other favorites that appear weekly or are a fixture in particular neighborhoods for fresh produce. Double check schedules before you go as they are often dependant on seasons. This is a great way to stock up on seasonal produce for less.

The Aventura Mall Farmer's Market
NE 196 St. & Biscayne Blvd. at the Aventura Mall Center Court, Aventura

From late April to October, this market is open on Sat from 10 a.m. to 9:30 p.m. and Sun from noon to 8 p.m.

Coconut Grove Organic Farmer's Market
3300 Grand Ave., Coconut Grove
(305) 238-7747

This market is open Sat from 10 a.m. to 7 p.m. Parking is sometimes tricky, so arrive early or expect to shell out a few bucks for a spot.

The Collins Park Sunday Market
22nd Street and Collins Avenue, Miami Beach

This market is open from 9 a.m. to 6 p.m. and includes local produce, baked goods, and usually free live music.

Lincoln Road Farmer's Market
Between Meridian Avenue and Washington Avenue on Lincoln Road, Miami Beach

There's an organic and green market every Sun from 9 a.m. to 6:30 p.m.

Norman Brothers Produce
7621 SW 87th Court, Kendall
(305) 274-9363
www.normanbrothers.com

Weekly specials are listed on their Web site, and don't miss their delicious shakes at the juice bar. Hours are 8 a.m. to 7 p.m. Mon to Sat and 9 a.m. to 6 p.m. on Sun.

Normandy Village Marketplace
900 Block of 71st St. at the Normandy Isle Fountain, North Miami Beach

This market, which offers mainly local produce and baked goods, runs every Sat from 9 a.m. to 5 p.m.

The Pinecrest Gardens Green Market
11000 SW 57th Ave. at Pinecrest Gardens, Pinecrest

This market runs through May from 9 a.m. to 2 p.m. on Sun.

Robert Is Here Fruit Stand and Farm
19200 SW 344th St., Homestead
(305) 246-1592
www.robertishere.com

Since 1960, Roberto has been a local favorite for healthy snacks. The stand is open 8 a.m. to 7 p.m. daily and closed in September and October.

Upper East Side Green Market
5556 NE 4th Court, NE Miami

Local produce, plants, eggs, and cheese are featured at this market, open Sat from 9 a.m. to 4 p.m.

Wayside Fruit and Vegetable
10070 SW 57th Ave., Coconut Grove
(305) 661-6717

The shakes here are a local favorite and all the produce is delicious. It's open Mon through Sat from 7:30 a.m. to 6 p.m. and Sun from 7:30 a.m. to 5:30 p.m. Watch your timing with the after school crowd.

FREE **SAMPLES** & **HAPPY** HOURS

Oodles of bars, pubs, clubs, and restaurants in the Miami area offer something free or cheap during happy hour. What you'll find runs the gamut from basic bar food (wings and potato skins) to tasty tapas (cheese, chorizo, etc.) to fine dining and discount shellfish. Love oysters but wince at their price tag? Don't fret—we've got some steals for you.

Sometimes you're expected to buy a drink to get the free nibbles, but happy hour is known for its drink discounts. No matter what, be sure to leave the bartender a nice tip, particularly if they've served you several free drinks. Yes, even cheap bastards should remember to tip. In this section we have only included those places that have a long history of offering free food and/or free drinks, but always call ahead to confirm—happy hour deals change as quickly as winds in a hurricane, and venues close down with a blink of an eye.

The Bar
172 Giralda Ave., Coral Gables
(305) 442-2730
www.gablesthebar.com

Sorry guys—this one is only free if you're female, but if you're lookin' to meet a gal, this might be cheaper than subscribing to an online dating Web site. Each Fri between 5:30 and 7:30 p.m., ladies drink free well drinks and Yuengling drafts in this dark, no-nonsense drinking den decorated with beer trays. This is a refreshingly attitude-free spot in swanky downtown Gables.

Foodie Events

Miami Spice
www.ilovemiamispice.com
From early August to late September, Miami has its version of restaurant week, which is absolutely the best time to take advantage of deals on fancy grub that you otherwise couldn't afford. Three-course meals are $22 for lunch and $35 for dinner. A few past highlight participants have included Emeril's Miami Beach Restaurant Bar also offering drink specials, Morton's the Steakhouse, and Shula's Steak House in Miami Lakes. Classy restaurants, including the Ritz-Carlton and the Setai, also participate. Also check the Web site for affiliated events that run throughout the months.

Miami Street Food Festival
Magic City Casino
450 NW 37th Ave., Opa-locka
http://miamistreetfoodfest.com
You won't find a lot of street food in Miami, but if you're a sucker for fast food that doesn't require a drive through, this is the place to be. Most recently held in October, you're guaranteed to find something tasty from local vendors.

South Beach Food and Wine Festival
www.sobewineandfoodfest.com
This is the big kahuna; the festival that attracts celebs out of the woodwork and, if you can find a ticket that doesn't break your bank account, will make you a savvy foodie for the rest of the year.

B.E.D. Restaurant and Nightclub
929 Washington Ave., Miami Beach
(305) 532-9070
www.bedmiami.com

What could be more elitist than an event titled "Secret Society" with free food as a bonus? Ladies will receive complimentary dinner from 10 to 11 p.m. every Mon with RSVP, which you can submit on the Web site.

Berries in the Grove
2884 SW 27th Ave., Coconut Grove
(305) 448-2111
www.berriesinthegrove.com

Another one for the ladies: Thurs is the night you won't want to miss—you'll drink free between 9 and 11 p.m. Not female? Happy hour drinks are half off for everyone from Mon to Fri from 4 to 7 p.m.

Boteco
916 NE 79th St., NE Miami
(305) 757-7735
www.botecomiami.com

Various nights of the week there is a half off happy hour that includes all house drinks. An added plus: complimentary appetizers are served. This typically runs from 5 to 8 p.m. Also check out Ladies Night specials on Tues from 7 to 11 p.m.

Botequim Carioca Brazilian Bar and Grill
900 Biscayne Blvd., Downtown Miami
(305) 675-1876

Just north of the main downtown financial district in a cluster of high-rise condos is this lively Brazilian bar. *Carioca* means a native of Rio, and if beach bums can't have fun, who can? Between 5 and 7:30 p.m., graze on the complimentary Brazilian apps like fried sausage with garlic, yucca croquettes, deep-fried Brazilian-style onion rings and coxinhas (chicken dumplings filled with cheese). Kick back with a few two-for-one caipirinhas. What's that you say? It's the national drink of Brazil: Cachaca (sugar cane liquor), muddled limes, sugar, and a splash of club soda.

Bougainvillea's Old Florida Tavern (Bougie's)
7221 SW 58th Ave., South Miami
(305) 669-8577
www.bougiesbar.com

Wed night the ladies drink free from 10 p.m. to 2 a.m., and to top it off, free live music accompanies those drinks. This is a great slice of old Florida in Miami, with low lighting, a mix of salty old locals, local college kids, and basically anyone seeking a fun evening with good ol' live music, Key West style.

The Cheese Course

3451 NE 1st Ave., Downtown Miami
(786) 220-6681
www.thecheesecourse.com

Free cheese tastings are offered throughout the year and vary by month. Try the tastiest flavors from around the world, which are typically paired with specialty wines. Also take advantage of free cheese classes. Call or check the Web site for schedules.

CJ's Crab Shack

1320 Ocean Dr., Miami Beach
(305) 534-3996
www.cjscrabshack.com

A front seat watching the Ocean Drive pretty people and parade does not get cheaper than this: $6 for a half-dozen oysters, $7 for two stone crabs. Top it off with $4 beer or $6 wine and cocktails (the cheapest drink you'll find at this address, we assure you), check out the Ferrari growling it's way past your table, and settle in for a fun but frugal evening.

Copas y Tapas

98 Miracle Mile, Coral Gables
(305) 774-0927
www.copasytapas.com

Between 4 and 6 p.m. each weekday, this tiny, cozy Spanish wine bar offers free tapas of one bite-nibbles like slices of chorizo or cubes of nutty manchego. Wash it down with two-for-one wine and beer from their Spain-focused drinks menu.

The DRB

255 NE 14th St., Miami
(305) 372-4565
www.drbmiami.com

Their Web site boasts a menu of over 400 beers from around the world, so it's not surprising that they creatively pair these during the DRB version of happy hour from 5:30 to 8 p.m. daily. Pre-selected six packs are available for fixed prices, which typically mean that you're saving the equivalent of a couple drinks. The cheapest "beer flight" is a combo of PBR, Miller, and other cheapies for $15. Selections go up from there and single beers can always be purchased.

Fox's Sherron Inn
6030 South Dixie Hwy., South Miami
(305) 661-9201

Step inside and you'll be transported to a romantic, old school speakeasy. The shady liquor window in the back is a great place to grab and go, but make time to sit down and focus on the solid appetizers and drink specials. Happy hour is two-for-one after 11 p.m. on Tues and Sat.

Fritz & Franz Bierhaus
60 Merrick Way, Coral Gables
(305) 774-1883
www.bierhaus.cc

This Austrian-Bavarian joint hosts a happy hour from 5 to 7 p.m. daily and offers half off appetizers and two-for-one drinks. If you're a schnitzel lover, don't miss the two-for-one night on Tues from 5 to 10 p.m.

Fuji Hana
111768 SW 88th St., Kendall
(305) 275-9003
www.fujihanakendall.com

Mon and Tues are dollar sushi nights—they even extend the special the rest of the week and the weekend between 5 and 7 p.m. Yup, take your pick from succulent pieces of fish and more sitting atop the rice (choose from the usual, such as salmon, eel, shrimp, tofu, and vegetables). We wouldn't call this place inventive, but at these prices, who cares? On Mon and Tues, try to get there before 8 p.m. to avoid a long wait—this special ain't much of a secret.

The Globe Café and Bar
377 Alhambra Circle, Coral Gables
(305) 445-3555
www.theglobecafe.com

Complimentary hors d'oeuvres, which are typically bites of cheese on tiny crackers and mini quiches, vary from day to day and circulate during happy hour from 5 to 7 p.m. Happy hours are Mon through Fri during the same hours and their happy hour for wine, titled WineOh! Tuesday, runs from 7 to 9 p.m.

Greenstreet Café
3468 Main Highway, Coconut Grove
(305) 444-0244
www.greenstreetcafe.net

The prime people-watching spot in the grove attracts us humans and celebrities, so if the sidewalk action dwindles, you might find yourself sitting next to A-Rod or some other glittery celeb. Happy hours (5 to 7 p.m. and 11 p.m. to closing) here are always packed and an excellent value ($6 martinis, $4.50 well drinks, $3.50 drafts and $2-off wines by the glass) but we really love Friday's free champagne for ladies (5 to 7 p.m.) and Mon's half-off all wine bottles all night.

Hofbräu Beerhall Miami
943 Lincoln Road, Miami Beach
(305) 538-8066
www.hofbraumiami.com

Two-for-one beer specials are offered on Wed from 5 to 7 p.m. at this local German favorite.

JoAnna's Marketplace
8247 South Dixie Hwy., South Miami
(305) 661-5777
www.joannasmarketplace.com

JoAnna's is one of Miami's most delicious specialty markets, so when there's a free tasting of food, wine, or anything else, you won't want to miss it. Check the Web site or call for updated schedules.

Hookah Me Happy

As a complement to your food and drink, there are quite a few hookah bars around the city, some with happy hours equivalent to drink specials.

D'vine Hookah Lounge
445 Lincoln Rd., Miami Beach
(305) 674-8525
www.dvinelounge.com
It's a puffer's paradise between 4 and 8 p.m., where the second shisha (the tobacco in a hookah) is free. No, not cigarettes, but hookahs, and not just any hookah: D'vine Hookah Lounge on Miami Beach's trendy Lincoln Road lets you puff flavored tobacco straight out of a fruit in an array of flavors. Order the watermelon and they plop the watermelon tobacco right into half of a watermelon at your table; order the pineapple and you get a pineapple. You get the picture. Just remember, one hookah is quite a bit of tobacco, so this is best shared with a group.

The Dilido Beach Club
1 Lincoln Rd. at the Ritz-Carlton, Miami Beach
(786) 276-4000
www.ritzcarlton.com
Hookah Lounge Happy Hour features complimentary hookah from 5 to 8 p.m. on Thurs and Fri.

Level 25
1395 Brickell Ave. at the Conrad Miami, Brickell
(305) 503-6529
www.conradmiami.com/level25

Hit up Wine Down Wednesday for a 50 percent off happy hour on all wines and champagnes. Also take advantage of $5 glasses of wine from 5 to 8 p.m.

Hookah Lounge
7400 SW 57th Ave., South Miami
(305) 668-3331
www.miamihookahlounge.com
Try their exclusive blends, including Mumbai Melon Mambo and Meso-
potamian Mercury. Check the Web site for a $5 off coupon that can be
used Mon through Thurs.

Layali Miami Mediterranean Restaurant and Hookah Lounge
11402 NW 41st St., Doral
(305) 403-0188
www.layalimiami.com
Take advantage of hookah happy hour Mon to Fri from 5 to 8 p.m.
featuring $8 hookah specials and drink specials. During other hours,
hookah costs $15, which isn't bad when split a few ways. They're open
11:30 a.m. to 10 p.m. Mon through Fri and until midnight on Sat.

Oasis Café
2977 McFarlane Rd., Coconut Grove
(305) 446-6565
oasiscoconutgrove.com
This is a Grove favorite, featuring $15 hookah from 9 a.m. to 6 p.m.
The price goes up after 6 p.m. (above $20!) so make sure to get there
early. Regardless, this spot is open late night, until 3 a.m. Thurs to
Sat and 1 a.m. the rest of the week.

Lush
233 12th St., Miami Beach
(305) 801-8301

It's rock n' roll meets a sports bar at SoBe's Lush. Wed is casino night, when
you can bet the bartender for the chance for a free drink. On Thurs ladies
drink free beer until 2 a.m. and you'll have until 5 a.m. to sober up or find
a ride home.

Mai Tardi

163 NE 39th St., Downtown Miami
(305) 572-1400
www.maitardimiami.com

Mai Tardi's Beat the Clock special is a budget diner's utopia: from 5 to 7 p.m. daily, the price varies according to the time the guest places the order. For example, order at 5:47 p.m., and you pay $5.47 for an entree. Enjoy the discounted Italian fare and pizzas straight from their snazzy pizza oven in the stylish terrace covered in trees and murals.

Mango's Tropical Café

900 Ocean Dr., Miami Beach
(305) 673-4422
www.mangostropicalcafe.com

Their happy hour is Mon through Fri from 4 to 7 p.m. and features two-for-one drink specials.

Monty's Stone Crab and Seafood

2550 South Bayshore Dr., Coconut Grove
(305) 856-3992
http://montysbayshore.com

Okay, this one ain't free, but Monty's is a local institution and offers one of the best raw bar specials in the city. Happy hour is between 4 and 8 p.m. on weekdays and offers half-off drinks and raw bar. Credit is given where it's due: half-off Florida stone crabs is no small feat. It's an outdoor bar, so expect a sturdy, expansive tiki bar and fab dance floor, usually featuring a live calypso or reggae band. The place gets jammed by 6 p.m., so come early to snag a seat. A Miami Beach location is at 300 Alton Rd. (305-672-1148, www.montyssouthbeach.com).

Morton's The Steakhouse

2333 Ponce de Leon Blvd., Coral Gables
(305) 442-1662
www.mortons.com

Yes, another chain it is, but this is one of Coral Gables' most popular upscale after work bars. And how can you resist their power hour, when drinks start at $4 and bar bites (think petite filet mignon sandwiches, mini crab cakes, and jumbo lump crab, spinach, and artichoke dip) only make you $5 poorer?

Mr. Moe's Restaurant and Bar
3131 Commodore Plaza, Coconut Grove
(305) 442-1114
www.mrmoes.com

On Tues nights, ladies drink free from 10 p.m. to 2 a.m., assuming the karaoke isn't too painful to listen to. There are drink specials daily, but some honorable mentions include $5 Jager Bombs during the 10 p.m. Beer Olympics Beer Pong Tournament on Mon night, $1 well drinks and domestic drafts on Tues from 10 p.m. to close, free drinks for ladies from 9 to 11 p.m. Wed night, and $4 martinis on Fri.

Nikki Beach
1 Ocean Dr., Miami Beach
(786) 515-1130
www.nikkibeach.com

The Catch: *This deal is conditional on entree purchases. So choose the cheapest thing on the menu.*

This trendy spot offers complimentary bottles of bubbly every Thurs from 6 to 9 p.m. with the purchase of two entrees.

Ortanique on the Mile
278 Miracle Mile, Coral Gables
(305) 446-7710
www.cindyhutsoncuisine.com

Free champagne tastings take place on Thurs from 5:30 p.m. until corks stop popping, which is usually around 6:30 p.m. as they open a limited amount of bottles. The crowds flock each week to this tropical Caribbean restaurant with mango walls bedecked with flower and citrus murals.

Paquito's Mexican Restaurant
16265 Biscayne Blvd., Sunny Isles Beach
(305) 947-5027
http://paquitosmiami.com

Aside from great grub, take advantage of happy hour on Mon through Thurs from 4 to 7 p.m., which includes two-for-one house margaritas, beer, and all house beverages. Freaky Friday, which takes places from 4 to 7 p.m. and 11 p.m. to midnight weekly, also features drink specials.

Peterbrooke Chocolatier

227 Aragon Ave., Coral Gables
(305) 446-3131
www.peterbrooke.com

On Thurs and Fri from 6 to 10 p.m., free wine and chocolate tastings take place. Also stop by on Wed, which is 99 Cent Gelato Day from 11 a.m. to 10 p.m.

Purdy Lounge

1811 Purdy Ave., Miami Beach
(305) 531-4622
www.purdylounge.com

This trendy spot has a ladies night on Thurs, when ladies drink free from 11 p.m. to 1 a.m.

The River Seafood and Oyster Bar

650 South Miami Ave., Brickell
(305) 530-1915
www.therivermiami.com

On Mon through Sat from 4:30 to 7 p.m., take advantage of half-off oysters and drink specials.

Sandbar Grove

3064 Grand Ave., Coconut Grove
(305) 444-5270
www.sandbargrove.com

Get a touch of the Florida Keys in this laid-back, Floribbean sports grill. Each Wed evening is penny beer night for drafts only. Plus, kids eat free between 4 and 10 p.m. And if that isn't enough, Hurricanes (the ubiquitous Florida rum-based cocktail) are half off all day. There's a special every day, but this one—and the half-off tacos all day Mon—is by far the best deal.

Sandbar Lounge Miami Beach
6752 Collins Ave., Miami Beach
(305) 865-1752

Free buffet is any cheap bastard's dream, so don't miss this one on Sun and Mon from 5 to 7 p.m. It's the usual—chicken nuggets, mozzarella sticks, and chips—but you can simultaneously relax in the laid-back Miami Beach sports bar and tavern with a Key West and island flair. Plenty of locals round out the crowd, even in high season.

Scarlett's Cabaret
2920 SW 30th Ave., Hallandale
(954) 455-8318
www.scarlettscabaret.com

Pun totally intended when I say "happy hour." This Hallandale strip club serves complimentary lunch on Mon through Fri from noon to 6 p.m. Happy hour is until 8 p.m. Tips are likely appreciated. Bring dollar bills.

Scully's Tavern
9809 Sunset Dr., South Miami
(305) 271-7404

This basic tavern has a kickin' free buffet spread between 5 and 7 p.m. Mon to Fri. Expect the usual pub grub like chicken tenders and quesadillas, chips and salsa, and for the healthy munchers, plenty of veggies with dip.

Sharp Shooters Billiards
7200 SW 117th Ave., Kendall
(305) 596-0588

The best thing about this place is not that you don't have to look cute to get in, but that you'll get free Bud draft while playing pool from 8 p.m. to 2 a.m. on Tues and Wed.

Sunset Corners Fine Wines and Spirits
8701 Sunset Dr., South Miami
(305) 271-8492

Nearly each week features a free tasting (sometimes with nibbles) with friendly commentary and information at this laid-back wine shop. Call or check out their Facebook page's events section to get info on the next free sipping event.

Sunset Tavern
7230 SW 59th Ave., South Miami
(305) 665-0606
www.delilane.com/sunset.php

Happy hours take place throughout the week and include half-off drinks and $1 beers, to name a few deals. Hours are Mon through Wed from 11 p.m. to 3 a.m., Thurs from 11 p.m. to 4 a.m. and Fri and Sat from 10 p.m. to 3 a.m. Expect a full house (mainly of UM students) during sporting events and weekend nights.

Tap Tap Haitian Restaurant
819 5th St., Miami Beach
(305) 672-2898

Between 5 and 7 p.m., this local institution—part restaurant, part art gallery, part cultural center—gives you half off their strong, well-mixed tropical rum cocktails and bar bites like malanga fritters (a root vegetable similar to taro) and grilled chunks of goat. It's a rarity to find such a fun, casual hangout in the thick of South Beach, and you can enjoy the atmosphere while admiring the vibrant murals gracing the walls, painted by a handful of well-respected Haitian artists.

Tapas y Tintos
448 Española Way, Miami Beach
(305) 538-8272
www.tapasytintos.com

This sexy tapas bar hosts happy hour weeknights, with two-for-one specials running Wed 4 to 7 p.m. and Fri 6 to 8 p.m. Thurs the specials run all evening, *mi amigo*, with two-for-one cava all night. The location is top-notch on the ultra-European am-I-in-Spain? street called, what else, Española Way, which is chock-full of dining and drinking nooks.

Tarpon Bend

65 Miracle Mile, Coral Gables
(305) 444-3210
www.tarponbend.com

Most happy hours end around 7 p.m., but here's one that thinks we ought to be happy—and frugal—from afternoon until night time, or perhaps all day. Mon through Fri from 3 to 9 p.m. and Sat until 7 p.m., all drinks are two-for-one. Fancy a taste of Cuba? Check in for Mojito Madness Thursday—it lasts all day and the fresh fruit flavors will only set you back $3.50. As if this wasn't enough, Wed night is ladies night, with two-for-one entrees (for ladies only!).

Tobacco Road Bar and Restaurant

626 South Miami Ave., Downtown Miami
(305) 374-1198
www.tobacco-road.com

Prices and timing during Tobacco Road's Fri happy hour change by a digit each year at Miami's oldest bar—nibble on free appetizers (the choice changes each week, but it tends to be basic like quesadillas or chicken tenders) with your 98 cent drink: Friday's happy hour lasts 98 minutes between

6 and 7:38 p.m., marking the bar's age (98 years in 2010). In 2011 they'll cost 99 cents for 99 minutes, lasting until 7:39 p.m.; in 2012 they'll go up to a buck for 100 minutes—you get the picture.

Town Kitchen and Bar
Plaza 57
7301 SW 57th Court, South Miami
(305) 740-8118
www.townkitchenbar.com

Each Thurs, ladies drink free champagne until 7 p.m. in this posh gourmet food joint. Best of all, it's *real* champagne, as in, made in Champagne, France—no sparkling wine impostors from Napa here. Men accompanying their cheap date get half off all drinks all day. Happy hour runs from 4 to 7 p.m. daily, including Sat, and features half off selected drinks. Keep your ears open for a late happy hour closer to the next day, too.

Twist
1057 Washington Ave., Miami Beach
(305) 53-TWIST (89478)
www.twistsobe.com

On Fri in the garden during happy hour, free BBQ is served with a likely side of drag. There's never a cover to get in.

Waxy O'Connor's
www.waxys.com and waxysmiami.com
690 SW 1st Court, Brickell area; (786) 871-7660
1248 Washington Ave., Miami Beach; (305) 534-7824
1095 SE 17th St., Fort Lauderdale; (954) 525-WAXY

Deals include $10 pizza and pint specials for Monday night football and $2 off all drinks on Fri. Various drink specials at every location are offered throughout the week.

BYO Beverage

BYO, or Bring Your Own, is a great way to save money on overpriced bottles. Thus, cheap bastards always love a good BYO joint.

Anacapri Italian Restaurant
2530 Ponce de Leon Blvd., Coral Gables
(305) 443-8388
www.anacaprifood.com
Take advantage of the waived corkage fees on Mon evenings.

Barbu
1935 West Ave., Miami Beach
(305) 532-3818
The organic tapas aren't the cheapest around, but you'll save loads on alcohol with a minimal $5 corkage fee.

Buena Vista Bistro
4582 NE 2nd Ave., Downtown Miami
(305) 456-5909
www.buenavistabistro.com
This classy BYO French joint has affordable entrees starting at $10. Fan favorites include the snapper, duck, and lamp chops. Check out the next door deli during the daytime for breakfast and lunch fare.

Green Gables Café
327 Alhambra Circle, Coral Gables
(305) 445-7015
www.greengablescafe.com
This health nut restaurant is vegan-friendly as well.

Lifefood Gourmet
1248 SW 22nd St., south of Brickell
(305) 856-6767
www.lifefoodgourmet.com
It's a raw food restaurant, so you're probably best off bringing wine that's organic or risk dirty looks. Plus, there's no corkage fee.

WINE **BARS**

There are a handful of wine bars in the city, many of which have wine-specific happy hours and tastings. Also take advantage of the **Coral Gables Wine Walk** (www.winewalk.net), which takes place periodically throughout the year. It costs $10 for each participating restaurant, which includes samples of wine and food at one venue. Gauge your tolerance, but the organizers suggest buying four tickets.

Automatic Slim's

1216 Washington Ave., Miami Beach
(305) 695-0795
www.automatic-slims.com

Any bar with a pole as a centerpiece inevitably gets sloppy by the end of the night. Thurs is 80s for ladies, when ladies drink free until midnight. There is no cover for anyone and other drink specials are offered throughout the week.

Bin No. 18

1800 Biscayne Blvd., Downtown Miami
(786) 235-7575
www.bin18miami.com

By the glass, wines here are as cheap as $6. There are also appetizers that are priced reasonably, including a French onion soup for $6.75 and pastas starting around $14. Open Mon through Sat from noon to midnight, reservations can be made online. Specials on Mon and Tues include bottles 50 percent off including a $12 malbec, $12 syrah, and $14 pinot grigio.

Cavas Wine Tasting Room

5829 SW 73rd St., South Miami
(305) 667-5332
www.mycavas.com

Take advantage of a 20 percent off discount with the purchase of any two bottles on Mon and Tues.

Club Sugar

2301 SW 32nd Ave., Coral Gables
(305) 443-7657
www.clubsugarmiami.com

This drag club offers free drinks on Sat from 10:30 to 11:30 p.m. I didn't say you won't have to fight to get to the bar, but if you make it, it's free!

El Carajo International Tapas and Wine

2465 SW 17th Ave., Coconut Grove
(305) 856-2424
www.elcarajointernationaltapasandwines.com

This wine-themed restaurant is open daily from 11 a.m. to 10 p.m. Don't miss their wine tastings on Fri and Sat from 5 to 8 p.m.

Happy Wine

5792 SW 8th St., West Miami
(305) 443-6070
www.happywinemiami.com

You can't go wrong with a wine shop that serves food 12 hours a day: 9 a.m. to 9 p.m. They do have tastings throughout the week and the best bet is to stop there for a pressed sandwich for lunch, taste test some glasses, then stock up on wine.

Layali Miami Mediterranean Restaurant and Hookah Lounge

11402 NW 41st St., Doral
(305) 403-0188
www.layalimiami.com

Hookah happy hour features $8 hookah, but don't forget the drink specials: $1 glass of wine for ladies, $4.50 premium drinks, and $3 imported and domestic beers from 5 to 8 p.m. Mon through Fri.

Out of the Blue Café and Wine Bar

2426 NE 2nd Ave., Downtown Miami
(305) 573-3800
www.outofthebluecafe.net

The best deal related to alcohol is a Sun brunch for $19.95 that runs from 10 a.m. to 5 p.m. weekly. A mimosa is included in brunch; there is also free Wi-Fi and delivery if getting out of bed is not an option.

W Wine Bar
3622 NE 2nd Ave., Downtown Miami
(305) 576-7775
http://winebarmiami.com

Wines start at around $7 by the glass and can be easily paired with anything on the reasonably priced menu. Various nights throughout the week feature a DJ and dancing.

Wine 69
6909 Biscayne Blvd., NE Miami
(305) 759-0122

Thursday night tastings are only $10, but there are other reasons not to miss this local favorite. The cheese selection, for one, and an extensive tapas-style menu and desserts.

FITNESS, FUN, & THE GREAT OUTDOORS:
CHEAP THRILLS

"Of course I have played outdoor games. I once played dominoes in an open air café in Paris."

—OSCAR WILDE

I will not convince you that Miami is an outdoor paradise, because it is a simple fact: Miami *is* an outdoor paradise. Beaches, parks, and plenty of space for outdoor activity are unparalleled. But any individual with even the slightest knowledge of Miami will ask the million-dollar questions: What about hurricane season? Or, what about the month of August when no hair product will combat frizzy-ness and no deodorant will keep you from developing giant sweat marks? That's where some of the indoor fun comes in; and that, too, is available in the city. Take advantage of the range of activities in the city, regardless of weather or sweaty-ness.

BEACHES

The upside: The further north you go, the less crowded and touristy you get. The downside: The further north you go, the fewer scantily clad people you're likely to see. Try 53rd to 63rd Street Beach or 21st to 35th Street Beach, both of which are walkable and accessible by the local 25 cent bus.

Each of these beaches is distinct and attracts crowds accordingly. Topless and nude sunbathing is permitted in some areas (Haulover Beach, specifically) but is unofficially discouraged in others because of the family atmospheres.

Bal Harbour
Beach Collins Avenue at 96th St., Bal Harbour

Try this beach if your goal is to get away from the trendiness and crowded-ness of South Beach.

Bill Baggs Cape Florida State Park
1200 South Crandon Blvd., Key Biscayne

There are walking and biking trails, as well as an historic lighthouse. There's also a parking fee that's $8 for two or more occupants and $4 for a single occupant.

Crandon Park
4000 Crandon Park Blvd., Key Biscayne

It's clean and gets a plus for particularly easy parking.

Haulover Beach
10600 Collins Ave., Bal Harbour

First things first: Do not visit Haulover if you have a problem with nudity. This is where you'll find it. But this beach is great for nudity and picnics . . . maybe not simultaneously.

Hobie Beach
North side of Rickenbacker Causeway, Key Biscayne

It's nicknamed Windsurfer Beach for a reason, so make sure to swing by if you're a fan. Also, rentals of water paraphernalia including jet skis and sailboats are available.

Lummus Park Beach
Ocean Drive between 5th and 15th Streets, Miami Beach

Volleyball lovers should visit this beach. Also, the best known gay beach is at 12th Street.

Matheson Hammock Park Beach
9610 Old Cutler Rd. between 93rd and 101st Streets, South Miami

Families and picnics are the usual here, but watch out for mosquitoes.

South Pointe Park
1 Washington Ave., Miami Beach

This park is ideal for city views, swimming, and picnicking.

Sunny Isles Beach
Collins Avenue between 163rd and 192nd Streets, Sunny Isles Beach

This beach is almost as far as you can get from South Beach and still be in Miami. But don't expect not to see any souvenir shops.

Surfside
Collins Avenue between 88th and 96th Streets, Surfside

Yet another South Beach escape that'll be a bit quieter than the rest of South Beach.

Island Hoppin'

Miami, and the beaches in particular, is a board game of Chutes and Ladders utilizing causeways to connect the handful of islands. Though many of the islands are homes of the rich and famous exclusively, others are accessible to the public and provide entertaining daytime getaways. Here are a few accessible options, and others that you'll just have to stare at unless you're a VIP.

Fisher, Hibiscus, Palm, and Star islands are too-expensive getaways, but they are fun to drive by and check out the massive homes. Al Capone was a Palm Island resident once upon a time; now various athletes, actors, and musicians are known to have homes there.

Pelican Island

(305) 754-9330

On weekends, take the free boat taxi from the 79th Street Causeway to this island, visible from the city. Expect barbecue parties, music, and, yes, pelicans. Call for boat schedules.

Watson Island

1050 MacArthur Causeway, between Miami and Miami Beach

(305) 350-7926

Easily accessible by car via the MacArthur Causeway, Watson is home to the Ichimura Miami-Japan Garden (p. 232), Miami Children's Museum (p. 142), and Jungle Island in addition to simply being a great scenic city lookout.

Virginia Key Beach Park

4020 Virginia Beach Dr., Key Biscayne
(305) 960-4600

There's a $3 entry fee per vehicle and it's open from 7 a.m. to sunset daily.

BOWLING

Bird Bowl
9275 SW 40th St., SW Miami
(305) 221-1221
www.birdbowl.com

This is the place to go if you want to get down and dirty, especially compared to the other swanky options in the city. Take advantage of the Morning Special on Sun from 8:30 a.m. to 11:30 a.m. (if you can get out of bed that early). Get an hour of free bowling when you buy an hour, which costs $20 per lane—not bad when you split it among four or more people. Wacky Wednesday from 7 p.m. to closing features games at $1.50 per game, per person. The $3 Thurs special features just that for games and shoes from 7 p.m. to closing. Shoes are always $3.50 to rent. Hours are Sun through Thurs from 8:30 a.m. to 1 a.m. and Fri and Sat from 8:30 a.m. to 3 a.m. Check the Web site for other specials.

Lucky Strike
1691 Michigan Ave., Miami Beach
(305) 532-0307
www.bowlluckystrike.com

The Catch: It's 21 and over only after 9 p.m. and there's an enforced dress code.

You think you know, but you have no idea. This place takes bowling from a germ-infested sport pastime and brings it to a whole new level. First, dress to impress when you go to this place. It's more like a nightclub with bowling than a bowling alley with trendy music. There are 20 lanes including 6 VIP lanes, bottle service, and free Internet among other amenities. Lanes cost $4.95 per game until 6 p.m. and $5.95 after that. Shoe rentals are always $4.95 and lanes can be rented at $9.95 per hour per person. Hours are Mon through Thurs from 11:30 a.m. to 1 a.m., Fri from 11:30 a.m. to 2 a.m., Sat from 11 a.m. to 2 a.m., and Sun from 11 a.m. to 1 a.m.

Splitsville

5701 Sunset Dr. at The Shops at Sunset Place, South Miami
(305) 665-LANE (5263)
www.splitsvillelanes.com

The Catch: After 8 p.m. a dress code and 21 and over age requirement are enforced.

This is another swanky bowling spot that's a bit more down to earth than Lucky Strike (not surprising as it's not on Miami Beach) but still ain't too shabby. Lanes are $2 on Tues after 9 p.m.; also take advantage of grub specials like $5 pizza and sushi on Tues and Thurs, respectively. Hours are Mon through Thurs from 4 p.m. to 2 a.m., Fri and Sat from 11 a.m. to 5 p.m., and Sun from 11 a.m. to 2 p.m.

PARK **IT** HERE!

There are dozens of parks all around Miami, most of which have playgrounds, sports fields, and paved trails for running, walking, and biking. Here are a few, but this is certainly not an exhaustive list. Check www.miamidade.gov for a full list of parks.

Biscayne National Park

9700 SW 328th St., Homestead
(305) 230-7275

Coral Reef Park
7895 SW 152nd St., Palmetto Bay
(305) 235-1593

Everglades National Park
Ernest Coe Visitor Center
40001 State Rd. 9336, Homestead
(305) 242-7700
www.nps.gov/ever

Fruit and Spice Park
24801 SW 187th Ave., Homestead
(305) 247-5727
http://fruitandspicepark.org

Haulover Beach Park
10800 Collins Ave., Miami Beach
(305) 947-3525

Matheson Hammock Park
9610 Old Cutler Rd., Coral Gables
(305) 665-5475

North Shore Open Space Park
Collins Avenue from 8th Street to 87th Terrence, Miami Beach
(305) 993-2032

South Pointe Park
1 Washington Ave., Miami Beach
(305) 673-7730

Rock Climbing

Rock climbing in Miami sounds like an oxymoron, but there is a place to do it that will be cheaper than a plane ticket to real mountains. **X-treme Rock Climbing Gym, Inc.** offers $15 day passes and $45 monthly memberships for unlimited climbing. Equipment rentals are $5 for climbing shoes, $3 for a harness, $1 for a chalk pack and belay device. Helmets are free, but you're better off with the $8 package deal for all the equipment. Another perk: free yoga classes are offered to members, which are $10 for visitors. Ask about discounts for students and current specials. The gym is located at 13972 SW 139th Court in West Kendall. Contact them at (305) 233-6623 or x-tremerock.com.

PICKUP **GAMES**

Infinite
Basketball, infinitehoops.com
Football, infinitefootball.com
Hockey, infinitehockey.com
Soccer, infinitesoccer.com
Softball, infinitesoftball.com

Due to schedules that constantly change, the best resource to find up-to-date pickup games in and around the city is the Infinite network. Use the search feature (type *Miami*) on the site specific to your sport.

Meetup
www.meetup.com

This is another great resource to find groups of people craving outdoor activities.

PUBLIC **POOLS**

These are some of Miami's pools that are open throughout the year, but remember: there's always the ocean! Many facilities offer swimming lessons. Hours vary by location and throughout the year, so call for current schedules or visit www.miamidade.gov/parks/facility-find_pool.asp.

AD Barnes Pool
3401 SW 72nd Ave., South Miami
(305) 665-1626

Goulds Park County Swimming Pool
19355 SW 114th Ave., SW Miami
(305) 233-5100

Marva Y. Bannerman Park
4830 NW 24th Ave., NW Miami
(305) 635-2461

Palm Springs North Pool
7901 NW 176th St., Hialeah
(305) 558-3762

Rockway Park
9460 SW 27th Dr., Sweetwater area
(305) 223-8769

Tamiami Park County Swimming Pool
11201 SW 24th St., Sweetwater area
(786) 315-5295

And here are a few pools that are only open during the summer.

Arcola Park
1680 NW 87th St., NW Miami
(305) 835-7987

Gwen Cherry Park NFL/YET Center

7090 NW 22nd Ave., NW Miami

(305) 694-4889

Helen Sands Pool

16350 SW 280th St., Homestead

(305) 248-1386

Little River Park

10525 NW 24th Ave., NW Miami

(305) 694-5121

Naranja Park

14150 SW 264th St., Naranja

(305) 258-1945 or (305) 258-4534 for the pool directly

Richmond Triangle Park

14375 Boggs Dr., Richmond Heights

(305) 274-9666

Tropical Estates Park
10201 SW 48th St., West Kendall
(305) 226-5782 or (305) 596-9324

YOGA

Cheap yogi bastards are in luck, because in Miami you'll never spend another penny (or very few) on yoga. In addition to the classes listed below, there are also classes on the sand at Third Street in South Beach, at 7 a.m. and 6 p.m. daily, for a $5 donation.

Bayfront Park
Tina Hills Pavilion, Downtown Miami

Free yoga classes take place at 6 p.m. on Mon and 9 a.m. on Wed and Sat.

Corpo Yoga Studio
9030 SW 72nd Court, Kendall
(305) 670-2010
www.corpoyogastudio.com

This studio offers free classes for first timers, which can be anything from Vinyasa to prenatal. Various classes are offered daily and throughout the week. A 15 percent discount is given to students for memberships.

Flamingo Park Yoga
Meridian Avenue and 13th Street, Miami Beach
(786) 444-1817

On Wed at 6 p.m. and Sat at 9:30 a.m., free yoga classes are held in Flamingo Park. Call Victoria Brunacci for more information and to check schedules; classes may be canceled on rainy days or holidays.

Kennedy Park
Bayshore Drive, Coconut Grove

At 9:30 a.m. there's a free yoga class every Sat.

Free Gym Offers

The outdoors is nice, but there's also hurricane season, 100 degree days, and mosquitoes. So if you're in the mood for a plain ol' gym, here are a few that offer a free trial for newcomers or fitness consultations.

24 Hour Fitness

2982 Grand Ave., Coconut Grove

(305) 448-2416

www.24hourfitness.com

Sign up for a free one-week pass on the Web site. Two more locations are at 350 Miracle Mile, Coral Gables (786-662-6764); and 8400 Mills Dr., Kendall (305-704-4540).

Crunch Gym

1676 Alton Rd., Miami Beach

(305) 531-4743

www.crunch.com

It may be a plain ol' gym, but it packs a punch with Cardio Striptease, Pole Dancing, and Virgin Yoga on the class schedule. This trendy see and be seen hot spot offers a free guest pass on the Web site for first time visitors. Traditional classes without sexual connotations are offered, including cycling, yoga, and Pilates. Also, ask about free consultations with personal trainers at all gyms. A second Miami Beach location is at 1259 Washington Ave. (305-674-8222).

Legion Park

6447 NE 7th Avenue, NE Miami

This park hosts free yoga classes that take place at 10 a.m. on Sat.

Gold's Gym

3737 SW 8th St., Coral Gables

(305) 445-5161

www.goldsgym.com

Sign up for a one-week pass on the Web site. Two additional locations are at 1400 Alton Rd., Miami Beach (305-538-GOLD); and 16357 NW 57th Ave., Miami Lakes (305-621-GOLD).

LA Fitness

900 South Miami Ave., South Miami

(786) 718-1750

www.lafitness.com

Go on the Web site to print a free one-day pass and check out the many other locations in the Miami area.

South Florida Fitness Group

14417 South Dixie Hwy., Palmetto Bay

(305) 233-9801

This cozy training gym is owned by trainer Tangy, who will kick your ass for free if it's your first time.

Lululemon Athletica

826 Collins Ave., Second Floor, Miami Beach

(305) 673-8496

The Catch: BYO mat and towel.

This trendy chain offers free classes on Sat at 10:30 a.m.

Pace Park
NE 18th Street and Biscayne Bay, Downtown Miami

Take a free class at 7 p.m. on Wed and 9:30 p.m. Sat.

Nomi Pilates
10295 Collins Ave. behind ONE Bal Harbour Resort, Bal Harbour
www.nomipilates.com

Yes, I know that yogis will argue it's not yoga, but it's close enough to put in this category! In fact, this studio also offers yoga, so we're even. This free fitness program is sponsored by the Village of Bal Harbour with a tax refund. Hooray! Classes are offered on Tues between 9 and 10 a.m. and on Fri and Sat from 10:30 to 11:30 a.m. for about 50 minutes each.

Oleta River Park
3400 NE 163rd St., North Miami Beach
(305) 431-1109 or (305) 919-1846

Every Sat at 9 a.m. there's a yoga slash mediation class for free.

Yoga in the Park
Bayfront Park
301 North Biscayne Blvd., Downtown Miami
(305) 358-7550

The Catch: BYO mat and towel.

Take advantage of outdoor, free yoga classes every Mon, Wed, and Sat for all levels.

Yoga in the Park (PAL)
Flamingo Park
11th Street and Jefferson Avenue, Miami Beach
(786) 444-1817

The Catch: BYO mat and towel.

The Miami Beach Police Athletic League (PAL) offers very cheap classes on Mon and Wed from 6 to 7 p.m. and Sat from 9:30 to 10:30 a.m. Classes run $20 for eight classes ($2.50 a class!), $10 for four classes, and $5 for single classes. Call instructor Victoria Brunacci for more information.

Yoga at North Shore Park
North Shore Park
501 72nd St., North Miami Beach

Another cheap yoga in a park offer, which typically takes place Mon from 11 a.m. to noon and Fri and Sat from 9 a.m. to 10 a.m. Register early in the month for $25 or take advantage of three classes for $10 or single classes for $5.

CHILDREN & TEENS:
OLLI OLLI OXEN FREE

"I've got seven kids. The words you hear most around my house are hello, goodbye, and I'm pregnant."

—DEAN MARTIN

If you're reading this section, you're in luck. Aside from specific activities and events tailored for kids, the majority of establishments in Miami (including museums and movies, to name a few) have free or discounted admission for children under certain ages. More often than not, deep discounts apply for children under 12 years old and very young children (shall we say "lap size"?) are regularly admitted for free. Always ask about discounts for children before purchasing tickets.

FAMILY **AFFAIRS**

Family events are common at various venues throughout the year. Check the full festival listing for a slew of other events suitable for the whole family. Below are a few that cater specifically to children.

Book Nook by the Bay
Deering Estate at Cutler
16701 SW 72 Ave., Palmetto Bay
(305) 235-1668
www.deeringestate.com

The Catch: The event is free, but only with paid admission to the site.

On the first Sat of each month, this event brings together the Deering Estate's Eco-Brigade and staff with the public for story telling, eco-friendly arts and crafts, and science programs. Admission for Deering Estate is $10 for adults and $5 for children ages 4 to 14.

Fabulous First Friday
Miami Science Museum
3280 South Miami Ave., Coconut Grove
(305) 646-4234
www.miamisci.org

The Catch: The telescopic viewing is conditional on the weather. Check the forecast, during hurricane season especially, before you go.

Beginning at 7:30 p.m. on the first Fri of every month, there's a free star show in the Planetarium. After that, from 8 to 10 p.m., the Weintraub Observatory opens for telescopic viewings.

Free Family Fun Days
The Historical Museum of Southern Florida
101 West Flagler St., Downtown Miami
(305) 375-1629
www.hmsf.org

On the second Sat of every month, the Historical Museum hosts this event from noon to 4 p.m. The free day includes museum admission and cultural events, which often include music and gallery tours. Recent themes have included Pirates of the Florida Shore and Florida's Flora and Fauna.

IDEA @ The Bass
Bass Museum of Art
2121 Park Ave., Miami Beach
(305) 673-7530
www.bassmuseum.org

Free family days take place on specific Sundays throughout the year from 2 to 4 p.m. Art projects, scavenger hunts, and free prizes and snacks are incentive enough to go—free museum admission is another.

Spring into Summer
Miami Children's Museum on Watson Island
980 MacArthur Causeway, Miami Beach
(305) 373-KIDS (5437)
www.miamichildrensmuseum.org

The Catch: Parking costs $1 per hour.

Yearly in May, there's a one day learning event at the museum, which is free and open to the public from 1 p.m. to 6 p.m. Browse the hands-on museum exhibits and enjoy free snacks and learning activities throughout the day.

Target Free Third Fridays
Miami Children's Museum on Watson Island
980 MacArthur Causeway, Miami Beach
(305) 373-KIDS (5437)
www.miamichildrensmuseum.org

Every third Fri of the year is another themed free day at the museum. Wild Animals and Hispanic Heritage have been highlighted in past events. The feature changes every month so kids will always enjoy new activities. Entrance and parking are free. The event is from 3 to 9 p.m.

FINE **ARTS,** FUN **CRAFTS**

Abrakadoodle
(305) 234-0006
www.abrakadoodle.com

Children's art classes are offered at several locations around the city through-out the week for various ages. Some classes carry a fee, like the painting program for 5 and 6 year olds at Sunset Elementary School, which costs $56 for a four-week session.

Artoconecto KIDSART
(786) 246-2047
http://artoconecto.blogspot.com

This Miami non-profit hosts a free Sat morning program for children ages 7 to 13. Local artists open their studios and participate in artist-led work-shops with themes including recycling or diversity. Art supplies are included as is lunch after the program at World Resources Café on Lincoln Road. Con-tact Danny Brody by phone or at artoconecto@gmail.com.

Kidflix Film Festival
www.kidflixfestival.com

Future film buffs should not miss this event. In April 2010, South Florida hosted its first film festival for kids ages 3 to 14. International films, animated features, and shorts were screened, in addition to activities in between screenings.

PLAYGROUNDS **&** OUTDOORS

Miami's layout may not be ideal for those who don't like cars, but it is ideal for a city full of play space. Beaches (in the Fitness, Fun, and the Great Outdoors chapter) are one good place to look, but there's nothing like a good ol' playground. Here are a few, but not even close to all that exist in the city. Check the city's Web site, www.miamidade.gov, for more listings and details. Unless otherwise indicated, most parks are open sunrise to sunset throughout the year.

Acadia Park
5351 NW 195th Dr., Opa-locka
(305) 621-2461

There is a basketball court and dog park on-site. The kid-friendly park also has a playground.

AD Barnes Park
3401 SW 72nd Ave., South Miami
(305) 666-5883

This is a 65-acre park that was opened in the late 1970s and hosts a variety of cultural activities. Visit the Nature Center open daily from 9 a.m. to 5 p.m., except Mon and Tues.

Amelia Earhart Park
401 East 65th St., Hialeah
(305) 685-8389

In addition to soccer fields and a dog park, there's a barn with a fully functioning petting area. Cows, goats, chickens, pigs, and sheep are among the animals there.

Belle Meade Mini Park
NE 8th Ave. at 77th St., North Miami

It's a mystery why they call it "Mini," as its size is fairly normal, but this park has a playground suitable for a variety of ages, picnic tables, and shade.

Bill Sadowski Park
17555 SW 79th Ave., Palmetto Bay
(305) 255-4767

The park itself is open daily except Mon and Tues from 9 a.m. to 5 p.m. A nature trail and bird-watching areas are on the property. Eco tours are offered but cost extra.

Coral Pine Park and Tennis Center
6955 SW 104th St., Pinecrest
(305) 668-7258

Open from 8 a.m. to 10 p.m. daily, this site has six lighted tennis course and fitness space for exercise and organized games.

Crandon Park Beach and Family Amusement Center
4000 Crandon Blvd., Key Biscayne
(305) 361-5421

The view itself is a worth a trip, but take advantage of the 2-mile beach and tennis and golf facilities as well.

Dante Fascell Park
8600 Red Rd., South Miami
(305) 666-8680

In addition to six clay tennis courts, there are handball and beach volleyball courts as well as a playground, all open sunrise to sunset.

El Portal Tot Lot
500 NE 87th St., El Portal
(305) 795-7880

Look for City Hall if you can't find this site, as its central location is behind the famous building. Picnic tables and open space are among the perks of this playground spot.

Enchanted Forest Elaine Gordon Park
1725 NE 135th St., North Miami
(305) 895-1119

The Catch: Okay, it's a pretty big one—a few sites report poisonous plants on-site. So beware.

There's an unpaved bike path, nature trail, and pony rides. With 22 acres, it's hard to go wrong and easy to stay away from the poisonous plants if you try.

Eureka Park
18320 SW 119th Ave., SW Miami
(305) 235-2151

Basketball and tennis courts are available on-site. Take advantage of the nearby Miami Metro Zoo.

Evelyn Greer Park
8200 SW 124th St., Pinecrest
(305) 234-2110

The playground has been named "Florida's best" by Parenting Magazine. Also take advantage of athletic fields, a wrap-around walking path, picnic tables, and free Wi-Fi.

Flagler Grove Park
7551 SW 104th St., Pinecrest

This three-acre park has lit soccer fields available for organized games and recreation, a playground, and plenty of open space.

Flamingo Park
999 11th St., South Beach
(305) 604-CITY (2489)

At over 30 acres, this park was reopened in 2005 and features a playground and football field and is still undergoing improvements. The City of Miami Dade lists three park entrances: 11th Street and Jefferson Avenue, 13th Street and Michigan Avenue, and 13th Street and Meridian Avenue.

Greynolds Park
17530 West Dixie Hwy., North Miami Beach
(305) 945-3425

A golf course and campgrounds are on-site. Join the hippie fest Love-In every May for free and fun activities at the park.

Hawthorne Tot Lot
Hawthorne Avenue and 90th Street, Surfside
(305) 866-3635

It's touted as one of the area's few shaded playgrounds, which is a big plus on a hot day. The modern playground and clean sandbox are two additional highlights.

Jefferson Reaves Senior Park (Brownsville Park)
3090 NW 50th St., Miami Springs
(305) 635-2081

There's a recreation center and tot lot in addition to lit shuffleboard and basketball courts

Jose Marti Park
351 SW 4th St., Little Havana

In addition to baseball and softball fields and multiple racquetball and basketball courts, this park has an on-site pool and classes offered throughout the year.

Kendall Indian Hammocks Park
11395 SW 79th St., Kendall
(305) 596-9324

It may not have the fancy courts and a pool like some other sites, but I give this park credit for its unique offering of a disc golf course. Baseball fields are on-site as well as picnic tables.

Normandy Isle Park
7030 Trouville Esplanade, Miami Beach

Amenities include a basketball court, soccer field, tot lot, adult lap pool, children's water playground, picnic pavilion, and recreation building.

Nuestras Raices and Hispanic Heritage Cultural Arts Center Park/Miller Drive Park
5510 SW 94th Court, Kendall
(305) 271-0812

It's a mouthful, but this park also offers a handful of activities including soccer, basketball, and tennis.

Ojus Park
18995 West Dixie Hwy., Sunny Isles Beach
(305) 931-5726

A basketball court is available for the public as well as a recreation center available for rent.

Olinda Park
2101 NW 51st St., NW Miami
(305) 633-4066

There are two lit basketball courts and a playground, though the park is closed Sun.

Palmer Park
6100 SW 67th Ave., South Miami
(305) 663-6319

Football and baseball fields are on-site in addition to a concession stand.

Peacock Park
2820 McFarlane Rd., Coconut Grove
(305) 442-0375

In addition to the playground, this park is a big draw as an event venue, including a yearly Fourth of July celebration.

Ron Ehmann Park
10995 SW 97th Ave., Kendall
(305) 271-3853

Soccer and softball fields and basketball courts are available in addition to a walking path.

Tropical Park
7900 SW 40th St. (Bird Road), Sweetwater area
(305) 226-8316

It's inevitable that this park is always busy with some activity. A tennis center, equestrian center, and amateur boxing program are on-site and the grounds are also open for playing and fitness. A dog park is also available.

Women's Park
10251 West Flagler St., Sweetwater area
(305) 480-1717

No, there is not a sign at the entrance that says "Women Only." It is simply a park that pays homage to the historic female contributions to the city with a women's history gallery and exhibit space for related shows.

STORYTELLING

Art of Storytelling International Festival
Miami Dade Public Library
101 West Flagler St., Miami
www.mdpls.org

This day-long family friendly storytelling event happens yearly around May. Aside from music, art, and a giant puppet theater, storytellers from all over the world will present throughout the day. The event is free for everyone. Check the Web site for dates and other storytelling events hosted by the library.

Barnes and Noble Turnoff Week
www.barnesandnoble.com

Every April, this bookstore hosts a week-long event at their stores around the country to celebrate activities that are alternatives to electronics. Storytelling and story time are big draws. Other performances, arts and crafts, and activities are offered as well. Check the Web site for a searchable list of events by store.

Book Nook by the Bay

Deering Estate at Cutler
16701 SW 72nd Ave., Palmetto Bay
(305) 235-1668
www.deeringestate.com

The Catch: The event is free, but only with paid admission to the site.

On the first Sat of each month, this event brings together the Deering Estate's Eco-Brigade and staff with the public for story telling, eco-friendly arts and crafts, and science programs. Admission for Deering Estate is $10 for adults and $5 for children ages 4 to 14.

Children's Alley Storytelling Stage at the Miami International Book Fair

Every November, this world-renowned book fair takes over Downtown Miami. The storytelling stage is a free festival feature and typically remains open from 10:30 a.m. to 6 p.m. the Fri through Sun of the event.

The Parent Academy Storytelling

Barnes and Noble
152 Miracle Mile, Coral Gables
(305) 995-2680
http://theparentacademy.dadeschools.net

Sat at 11:30 a.m. The Parent Academy offers free storytelling for children of all ages year-round. A second storytelling venue is at 12405 North Kendall Dr. at the West Kendall Barnes and Noble.

SUMMER CAMPS

Yes, the heat is brutal, but what kid wouldn't want to spend the summer in a swimsuit outdoors? If the tourist bureau revamps its campaign to attract visitors to the city, the wealth of summer camp options (and many free or extremely cheap, at that!) should be highlighted. In some cases, there is a slight catch: many of the "free" programs are funded by organizations (such as The Children's Trust), which only provide a certain number of free slots before a fee is required. Unless specified, these slots are available on a first come, first served basis so sign up early!

AileyCamp
Adrienne Arsht Center for the Performing Arts
1300 Biscayne Blvd., Downtown Miami
www.alvinailey.org

You've heard of the famous Alvin Ailey in New York; this is a Miami version for kids. The camp, which is free, targets students with "academic, social, and domestic challenges"; emphasizes positivity; and includes curriculum of all types of dance. Yes, I did say free, but admission is selective based on background. (Free includes all activities, uniforms, field trips, breakfast, and lunch.) Roughly 80 students are selected who are currently 11 through 14. The Miami 2010 dates were late June through early August, but may change by year. To apply, contact (786) 468-2270 or education@arshtcenter.org.

AMC Summer Movie Camp
www.amcentertainment.com/smc

Every summer specific AMC theaters open their doors for a Summer Movie Camp that typically runs from June through August. The "camp" is actually a Wed show that typically plays at 10 a.m. for $1. The 2009 movie schedule included *Kung Fu Panda, Madagascar: Escape 2 Africa, Tale of Despereaux,* and *Horton Hears a Who.* All movies are kid friendly. Also take advantage of snack deals: $3 for a KidsPack, including a small drink, popcorn, and snack, which is regularly $5.75.

Art South Cultural Arts Center
240 North Krome Ave., Homestead
(305) 247-9406
www.artsouthhomestead.org

The Creative Arts Summer Camp is targeted to kids ages 7 to 18 and highlights visual and performing arts including drawing, painting, clay, improv, and more. Tuition is $60 per student per week in two-week blocks.

Aventura Learning Center
2221 NE 171st St., Aventura
(305) 940-0408
http://aventuralearningcenter.com

The summer camp component of this center, which offers year-round after school care for $150 per month, focuses on music, arts, and crafts and includes field trips.

Baseball Camp
Shenandoah Park
1800 SW 21st St., Miami
(305) 644-8888
www.miamigov.com/cms/parks

The Kiwanis Club of Little Havana has sponsored this free summer Baseball Camp for 15 years. It's open to kids ages 7 to 13. Call for more information.

Basketball Camp
Booker T. Washington High School
1200 NW 6th Ave., Homestead
(305) 416-1372
www.miamigov.com/cms/parks

Aspiring 14- to 17-year-old basketball stars should sign up for this June through August summer camp. Typical times are 9 a.m. to 3:30 p.m.; the $25 registration fee covers the first two weeks and each additional week is $10. Call Jose Diaz for more information.

Breakthrough Miami/College Bound
3747 Main Highway at Carrollton School of the Sacred Heart, Coconut Grove;
(305) 781-7622
http://breakthroughmiami.org

I'm not sure why 10-year-olds can enroll in a college prep program, but it's Miami and anything is possible. This no-fee camp caters to 13- to 16-year-olds at the Carrollton School and 10- to 13-year-olds at Ransom Everglades (2045 South Bayshore Dr., Coconut Grove, 305-781-5403). Educational courses are highlighted most and special interests, be it arts or debate, are encouraged.

City of Homestead Summer Camp
Homestead Sports Complex
1601 SE 28th Ave., Homestead
(305) 224-4570
www.cityofhomestead.com

Arts and crafts, sports, and weekly field trips are what's going on at this camp for 6- to 13-year-olds. Registration is $10 and the weekly fee is $80 per week for local residents. Discounts are offered, including $5 off per sibling and a $200 flat fee if paying three weeks at a time.

City of Miami Parks and Recreation Summer Camp Program
Jose Marti Park
351 SW 4th St., Downtown Miami
(305) 579-6958
www.miamigov.com/cms/parks

The City of Miami has done something right: their Summer Camp Program is available at over a dozen parks around the city for kids ages 7 to 13. Listed parks, only a few of the bunch, have pools on-site. Check the Web site for registration details. Other locations include, but are not limited to: Morningside Park, 750 NW 55th Terrace, Little Haiti (305-754-1242); Range Park, 525 NW 36th St., NW Miami (305-757-7961); and Virrick Park, 3255 Plaza St., Coconut Grove (305-445-0160).

Cool Kids Learn
Frank C. Martin K-8 Center
14250 Boggs Dr., Richmond Heights
(305) 826-9595
http://coolkidslearn.com

A special leadership and fitness program exists here for 11- to 14-year-olds. Registration is $20 and tuition is $50 per week.

Fairchild Tropical Botanic Garden
(305) 258-0464, ext. 309
www.fairchildgarden.org

This free of charge summer camp specializes in outdoor art and exploration for children ages 6 to 10. The dates are typically early or mid-July to early August.

Kayleen's Learning Center
10855 SW 72nd St., Suite 30, Kendall
(305) 274-5553

Children ages 5 to 12 can attend this program for $20 per week that includes homework help and recreational skills.

Miami Police Athletic League (PAL) Summer Camp
400 NW 2nd Ave., Downtown Miami
(305) 603-6088
www.palmiami.com

This organization offers a free summer camp every year featuring sports (basketball, tennis, swimming . . . you name it!) and field trips.

Shake-A-Leg Miami
2620 South Bayshore Dr., Coconut Grove
(305) 858-5550, ext. 119
www.shakealeg.org

Summer camp programs are for children ages 6 and above. Outdoor activities as well as academics are offered.

Super Camp
Curits Park
1901 NW 24th Ave., NW Miami
(305) 634-4961
www.miamigov.com/cms/parks

This is a slight step up from summer camp but is still pretty cheap. Starting at $60 per week for residents (after a $25 registration fee), the perks of this program include a strict ratio of campers to counselors and an early drop off option at 7:30 a.m. as well as late pick up at 6 p.m. for $10 extra per week. Field trips and daily activities are included in the general fee. Three additional locations include: Robert King High, 7025 West Flagler St., West Miami (305-261-6151); Shenandoah, 1800 NW 21st Ave., NW Miami (305-856-9551); West End, 250 SW 60th Ave., Miami (305-264-0341).

Tennis Camp
Bryan Park
2301 SW 13th St., near Little Havana
(305) 642-1271
www.miamigov.com/cms/parks

Yet another freebie by the City of Miami, this tennis program is open to kids ages 7 to 13. They typically take a maximum of 60 campers so call early to reserve a spot.

Urgent, Inc.

5202 University Dr., 315 Merrick Building, Coral Gables
(305) 576-3048
http://urgentinc.org

Girl-only programs cater to 6 to 13-year-olds and highlight cheerleading, dance, arts, swimming, social skills, and more. After a $30 registration the weekly fee is only $20. Transportation to and from Overtown is available to the University of Miami location.

WeCare of South Dade

South Dade Weed and Seed, Inc.
600 SW 14th St., Miami
(305) 224-5590

Children ages 6 to 17 are welcome at this summer camp, which includes swimming lessons, field trips, arts and crafts, and reading help. The fee is $20.

YOUTH **CENTERS**

They aren't always cheap to join, but they do offer a slew of programs, activities, and events for children. If nothing else, these are great options for rainy days. Many of these centers have extravagances including ice rinks and full gyms. Call in advance and/or check the Web sites for details on upcoming events and deals.

Allen Park/DeLeonardis Youth Center

1770 NE 162nd St., North Miami Beach
(305) 948-2927
www.citnmb.com

This center has various programs and activities, including co-ed boxing as well as a sports and youth program. Center hours are Mon through Fri from noon to 9 p.m. and Sat from noon to 5 p.m. The center is closed on Sunda.

Jorge Mas Canosa Youth Center

250 SW 114th Ave., Sweetwater
(305) 551-4774

This center is most notably a host for children's programs, including karate, dance, and basketball, among others. Those activities typically run from 5 to 8 p.m. throughout the week. The center itself is open at 9 a.m. daily. Call for information on current programs.

Miami City Mission Youth Center

3027 NW 7th St., NW Miami
(305) 633-5105

Children get in free at this center, which is more like a gym than a youth facility. Hours are 5:30 a.m. to 8 p.m. daily. Take advantage of the low fees, which are $50 for the first month of membership and $25 per month for each month thereafter.

North Shore Park and Youth Center

501 72nd St., Miami Beach
(305) 861-3616

This youth center includes a gym that is open from daily from 9 a.m. to 8 p.m. Other facilities include a game room open Wed from 9 a.m. to 1 a.m., Sat 8:30 a.m. to 5 p.m., Sun from 8:30 a.m. to 11:30 a.m., and at varied hours throughout the year. A computer lab is also available. Call for details about programming and current schedules.

Overtown Youth Center

450 NW 14th St., Overtown
(305) 349-1204
www.overtownyouthcenter.org

This neighborhood does not have the best reputation, but this center, sponsored by Alonzo Mourning's charity, is definitely one to check out. Programming includes activities and specialized camps throughout the year. Call for current schedules.

Pridelines Youth Services

9526 NE 2nd Ave., Suite 104, Miami Shores
(305) 571-9601
www.pridelines.org

This youth center caters to GLBTQ youth and offer a safe place for questions and advice. Various events are hosted year-round, at the facility and elsewhere. Check the Web site for current schedule details.

Scott Rakow Youth Center
2700 Sheridan Ave., Miami Beach
(305) 673-7767
http://web.miamibeachfl.gov

This hidden treasure features a pool, ice rink, and fitness center among other entertaining activities and programs.

South Miami Youth Center
5800 SW 66th St., South Miami
(305) 668-7389

For a rainy day, this is a great spot for indoor sports including basketball, flag football, and Wiffle Ball, among others.

War Memorial Youth Center
405 University Dr., Coral Gables
(305) 460-5620
www.coralgables.com

This Gables center has a handful of programs throughout the summer and year-round that range from dance and art to sports and performing arts.

AFTER **SCHOOL** PROGRAMS **&** TUTORING

Let's be honest: It's a recession. Parents have to work most of the year and unless your kid is a dedicated bookworm and every day is Take Your Child to Work Day, you must entertain them somehow. Summer camp tuition and after school programs are no joke, but the city provides a variety of free or subsidized programs that parents should take advantage of. Almost any school or cultural center in Miami offers programs for kids year-round. For cheap (or broke) adult bastards, here are a few that will appeal to you (and your pocket) for your kids.

Keep in mind, while many of the tuition fees that are either extremely minimal or nonexistent are real, most of them come in limited quantities. The **Miami Children's Trust** (www.thechildrenstrust.org) sponsors many of the subsidized tuition offerings and they are typically awarded on a first come, first served basis. This is only a fraction of the available programs, so if you feel overwhelmed by this list alone, contact the Miami Children's Trust by phone at (305) 854-0162 or visit their Web site for a comprehensive listing breakdown. This also applies to summer camps, which are listed in the section below.

After School Program
www.miamigov.com/cms/parks

Over a dozen spots around the city are included in the City of Miami's free and paid after school programs. They run from 2 to 5 p.m. for children ages 7 to 13. Homework assistance is available at some locations, while others encourage outdoor activities, and others team sports. Call the specific park you're interested in for more information.

The Bertha Abess Children's Center
1420 Washington Ave.
Fiendberg-Fisher Elementary School, Miami Beach
(305) 756-7116
http://baccinc.org

This no-fee camp is tailored for children ages 5 to 14 with disabilities and includes summer camp and after school programs throughout the year. Call for information on additional sites and schedules. Two more locations are at 2225 NW 103rd St. at Miami Park Elementary School, NW Miami and 29035 SW 144th Ave. at Irving and Beatrice Peskoe Elementary School, SW Miami.

Boys and Girls Clubs of Miami Dade, Inc.
1200 Michigan Ave., Miami Beach
(305) 673-7760
http://bgcmia.org

The Boys and Girls summer camp costs merely $35 for an eight-week session. Two groups are available of 5- to 8-year-olds and 9- to 13-year-olds.

Catholic Charities Notre Dame Child Care Center

130 NE 62nd Street, Little Haiti; (305) 751-6778
http://ccadm.org

This after school program is free of charge and tailored for children ages 5 to 12. Focuses are on arts and social skills. A second location is at 28520 SW 148th Ave., Homestead (305-245-0979).

Cool Kids Learn

14580 SW 117th Avenue at Glendale Church, Homestead
(305) 826-9595
http://coolkidslearn.com

This organization offers a tailored leadership and fitness program for children in sixth to eighth grade, regardless of age. Registration is $20 and tuition is $20 per week. A second location is at 23555 SW 112th Ave. at Goulds Elementary School, SW Miami.

Girl Scout Council of Tropical Florida, Inc.

505 SW 8th St.
Laura C. Saunders Elementary, Homestead
(305) 253-4841
www.girlscoutsfl.org

The Catch: None really, but a $5 per week donation is accepted.

These free after school programs offered by the Girl Scout Council are tailored for ages 5 to 12 years old and offer tutoring services as well as fitness and leadership activities. A second location is at 1550 SW 6th St. at West Homestead Elementary, Homestead.

Learn to Swim

(305) 638-8340
www.miamigov.com/cms/parks

There are about a dozen pools affiliated with this year-round City of Miami program, which is open to toddlers above two up through adults. After completing the 10-session course, Red Cross Certification is given to all participants. The fee is only $35 per eight sessions for city residents ($45 for non-city residents) that includes two sessions weekly for a month. For more information call Hadley Pool at the listed number.

Lincoln Marti Community Agency
28800 SW 152nd St.
South Miami Dade Campus, Homestead
(305) 643-4888, ext. 226
http://lincolnmarti.com

This no fee after school program is for kids ages 5 to 13 living in Little Havana and Leisure City. Outdoor and academic activities are offered, including art and tutoring.

Miami Learning Center
2780 SW 37th Ave. Suite 200, near Coconut Grove
(786) 270-0562
http://miamilearningcenter.net

All Florida schools require that children take and pass a standardized test affectionately known as the FCAT (Florida Comprehensive Assessment Test.) This after school program offers FCAT test preparation for children ages 5 to 17. Homework help and academic tutoring in various subjects are also available. Fees are on a sliding scale.

Neytz haChochma, Inc.
21101 NE 26th Ave.
Aventura Waterways K-8 Center, Aventura
(305) 945-7443
http://neytz.com

I can't pronounce the name either, but this center offers after school programs on a sliding scale, which is typically in the range of $25 to $100 per week. The focus is on children with special needs and integrating them back into mainstream schools.

S.M.A.R.T. Program (Science, Math, and Reading Tutoring)
(305) 375-3563
www.mdpls.org

The Miami Dade Public Library offers a free tutoring program during the school year at all branch libraries. Registration for the next school year is on a first come, first served basis, typically in early June. Sessions are one hour maximum and most branches offer the program Sat at 10 a.m., 11 a.m., and noon. A few libraries have alternative hours, including the Model City

Branch library on Wed from 4 to 6 p.m. and the Miami Lakes, West Dade Regional, and West Kendall libraries, which offer additional hours on Sat from 2 to 5 p.m. Call to sign up.

Shake-A-Leg Miami
2620 South Bayshore Dr., Coconut Grove
(305) 858-5550, ext. 119
www.shakealegmiami.org

After school programs are free and cater to kids ages 7 to 12. Outdoor and academic enrichment in various subjects are offered, using Biscayne Bay as an outdoor classroom.

South Florida After School All Stars
14950 SW 288th St. at Leisure City K-8, SW Miami
(305) 576-4026
www.afterschoolallstars.org

Children 11 to 16 can attend this after school program free of charge. Field trips, arts, and daily snack included!

South Florida Youth Sports
(305) 600-8701
www.southfloridayouthsports.com

This program offers cheerleading, dance, tennis, karate, and other classes for kids. They allow you to sign up for a free class and classes are only $35 to $40 per month anyway.

WeCare of South Dade
1515 Redland Rd., Florida City
(305) 247-9693
wecareofsouthdade.org

These free of charge after school programs are for children from 5 to 18 based on location. Galata, Inc. caters to 11 to 18 year olds and highlights reading, physical fitness and various arts and cultural activities. The Haitian-American Organization of Women location (305-245-8158) and Little Kingdom (700 NW 10th Ave., NW Miami, 305-431-2835) are for kids ages 5 to 13 and 5 to 12, respectively. Ages 6 to 13 are welcome at the South Dade Weed and Seed location (600 SW 14th St., Miami) for homework help, outdoor activities, and field trips.

YMCA of Greater Miami
18600 West Dixie Highway at Ojus Elementary, SW Miami
(305) 357-6622
http://ymcamiami.org

This after school program for kids ages 4 through 12 includes homework help, arts, and sports activities. Registration is $40 and the fee is $40 per week. The weekly fee for the West Homestead Elementary location is only $36. Check the Web site for a comprehensive listing of locations and programs.

EDUCATION:
YOU'VE GOT CLASS

"I took the speed reading course and read War and Peace in twenty minutes. It's about Russia."

—*WOODY ALLEN*

There are plenty of creative juices flowing in Miami and the classes offered around the city reflect this. Many educational institutions offer adult non-credit classes, so anyone can easily access his or her artistic side. Painting, DJig, photography—you name it. Here are a few existing options, but a simple google search may also yield results as schedules change seasonally and new classes pop up frequently.

ARTS & MEDIA

Art Atelier
14101 South Dixie Hwy., Suite K
2nd Floor in The Falls, Kendall
(786) 553-3331 or (305) 432 4034
http://artclassesmiami.com

The Catch: Classes are a little pricey after the first free lesson and supplies are not included.

Take advantage of a free first class, especially because after that's it's not anywhere close to free ($60 for a three-hour workshop and $50 for two hours). Painting classes for kids run Mon, Wed, and Fri after 3:30 p.m. and adult classes are held Tues and Thurs from 10 a.m. to noon Check their Web site for other creative workshops throughout the week.

Color Me Mine
5701 Sunset Dr., South Miami
(305) 665-0646
www.colormemine.com

It's not exactly an art class, but the staff is typically art-savvy and will help you with paint designs. It's normally not a cheap activity, but specials are offered throughout the week including free and discounted studio fees. Two other locations are at The Falls Mall, 8888 SW 136th St., Suite 507, Kendall (305-233-9323); and 19575 Biscayne Blvd., Suite 3201, Aventura (305-931-4470).

Miami Dade College
(305) 237-0651
www.mdc.edu

Various non-credit classes are offered at Miami Dade for adult enrichment. Music, art, and photography classes are among the selections, which typically run about $100 for a month-and-a-half course that meets once or twice a week. Typically, supplies are included or a small fee is required.

Scratch DJ Academy
2 NE 40th St., Suite 304, NE Miami
(305) 535-2599
www.scratch.com

Aspiring DJs (or anyone who secretly wants to be one) can take a free one-hour course at this academy. They offer free sample courses of DJing and Beat Making. Call or check the Web site for details and more information.

BODY & MIND

See the Fitness, Fun, and the Great Outdoors chapter for information on free yoga classes and the Dance chapter for information on free dance classes for first timers.

Public Libraries

The Miami Dade Public Library System includes multiple locations across the city. (See Appendix D for a complete listing). Free books are among the benefits of being a member, but members and non-members alike can take advantage of many events and services at the library. Check **www.mdpls.org** or call the individual branches for more information.

Drag It Out

Sailboat Bend Artists Lofts
1310 SW 2nd Court Suite 103, Fort Lauderdale
(954) 612-4489
www.dragitout.org

You are bound to be artistically enriched with 10 weeks of free gender impersonation classes. This non-profit hosts these classes on a volunteer basis, which culminates in public performance. Most recently classes have included Kings Class with Rico Suave, Queen/Bio Class with Twat LaRouge and Chocolatta, and Kings Class with DeVon Scamp. Classes are once per week from 7:30 p.m. to 10:30 p.m. To sign up, call Tabatha Mudra.

Fist

2275 NE 164th St., North Miami Beach
(305) 405-2001
www.fistma.com

Free trial classes are offered for adults and children. Call for availability.

Kukuwa Dance Workout

17051 NE 19th Ave., North Miami Beach
(305) 491-1445
www.kukuwadanceworkout.com

I'm not sure if this is humanly possible, but I'd go to this just because of their claim that you burn 970 calories in a 60-minute class. It's a blend of Latin, African, and Caribbean and apparently will result in your weight loss. Classes are advertised for $5 each.

Meditation Miami

(305) 891-9933
www.meditationmiami.com

Classes are offered at various venues around the city and are typically completely free or extremely discounted. In addition to meditation, expect elements of breathing work and yoga as well. Check the Web site for current courses and schedules.

¿Habla Inglés?

It probably doesn't surprise anyone that one of the most frequently offered academic classes in the city that are free or cheap are English language classes. Often referred to as English as a Second Language (ESL) or English for Speakers of Other Languages (ESOL), these classes are often offered at community centers, schools, and in various venues around the city.

Adult and Career Technical Institute
Miami Dade Public Schools
(305) 558-8000
http://freeenglishclasses.net
A variety of locations and schedules are available. Call or check the Web site for more information.

Biscayne Community and Adult Education Center
800 77th St., Miami Beach
(305) 868-7727
This is one option for free classes to learn or improve your English. Classes are typically Mon through Thurs from 6 to 9 p.m. Take advantage of the free child care program while attending this particular class.

Miami Dade College
300 NE 2nd Ave. at the Wolfson Campus, Downtown Miami
(305) 237-7369
www.mdc.edu
This local college offers free ESOL classes as well as citizenship education classes. Some locations offers GED completion classes as well. The catch—the class is free, but the books are not. Check the MDC Web site for more campus locations.

Oleta River Park

3400 NE 163rd St., North Miami Beach
(305) 431-1109 or (305) 919-1846

Every Sat at 9 a.m. there's a yoga slash meditation class for free.

PGA Free Lesson Month

Palmetto Golf Course
9300 SW 152nd St., Palmetto Bay
(305) 238-2922
www.playgolfamerica.com

Take advantage of free lessons and family clinics at select courses around the city each May. Check the Web site for details and valid locations, including the Calusa Country Club, 9400 SW 130th Ave., Kendall (305-386-5533); and the Biltmore Golf Course, 1210 Anastasia Ave., Coral Gables (305-460-5364).

Police Athletic League (PAL) Fitness Classes

999 11th St., Miami Beach
(305) 531-5636

PAL offers a variety of fitness classes, which are free for members and only $5 each for non-members. Abs and salsa cardio are a few of the past classes offered for this minimal fee. Yoga is also offered on Wed and Sat from 6 to 9 p.m.

Water Aerobics

11th Street and Jefferson Avenue at Flamingo Park Pool, Miami Beach

On Mon and Thurs from 7 to 8 p.m., free water aerobics classes are offered for residents. It's $6 for non-residents. Despite the mild Miami winter, the pool is heated above 80 degrees.

Yee's Hung Ga International Kung Fu Association

1822 NW 38th Ave., Lauderhill
(305) 790-1765
www.yeeshunggamiami.com

The Catch: Students must be a minimum of 18 years old and no walk-in students will be accommodated.

Free trial classes are offered to new students. Call Sifu Wilson Gomez for more information. The facility is open daily from 5 to 11 p.m. Mon through Fri and 10 a.m. to 1 p.m. on Sat and Sun.

DIGITAL **DOMAIN**

Elevate Miami Computer Classes
Jose Marti Park
351 SW 4th St., Downtown Miami
(305) 575-2103
Elevate Miami main number: (305) 416-1538
www.elevatemiami.com

Lab hours and classes are offered free of charge at five locations through Elevate Miami. Computer basics, Microsoft, and more advanced web-based classes are available. Call the individual locations or Elevate Miami directly for more information. Other locations include Curtis Park, 1901 NW 24 Ave., Miami (305-634-4961); Reeves Park, 600 NW 10th St., Overtown (305-579-6970); Ambrister Park, 236 Grand Ave., Coral Gables (305-442-0376); and the Sisters and Brothers Forever Senior Center, 1925 SW 8th St., Little Havana (305-631-0700).

Miami Dade Public Library Computer Lab

North Dade Regional Library
2455 NW 183 St., Miami Gardens
(305) 375-2044
www.mdpls.org

Free beginner computer classes are offered at two locations. Call in advance to sign up. Second location is at the South Dade Regional Library, 10750 SW 211 St., Cutler Bay (305-233-8140).

The Parent Academy

(305) 995-2680
http://theparentacademy.dadeschools.net

This organization offers free computer classes on Tues and Thurs from 6 to 10 p.m. during the school year, which runs from August to May. Call to sign up and reserve a spot.

RESEARCH **CENTERS**

Research centers are typically open to the public and free. Aside from libraries, to state the obvious, museums often have in-depth archives available to visitors. Some centers and archives are free for residents, but charge a fee for visitors from other states.

The Black Archives, History and Research Foundation of South Florida, Inc.
5400 NW 22nd Ave., Building C, Suite 101, NW Miami
(305) 636-2390
www.theblackarchives.org

This extensive archive preserves history since 1896 and is open to the public. A searchable database on the Web site allows users to view what's in the collection.

The Bramson Archive
(305) 757-1016
www.sethbramsonbooks.com

The Bramson Archive is privately owned and the largest collection of Florida East Coast (FEC) railway and Florida transportation memorabilia in the world. In addition, it is the largest private collection of Miami memorabilia and Floridiana in America. There is no charge for a visit but appointments must be made in advance via phone between 9:30 a.m. and 9:30 p.m.

Brockway Memorial Library
10021 NE 2nd Ave., Miami Shores
(305) 758-8107
www.brockwaylibrary.org

Aside from being the local library, it is also affiliated with the Miami Shores Archives Room, which contains all you need to know about Miami Shores history and additional information about the county and state. Hours are Mon, Tues, and Thurs from 9 a.m. to 8 p.m., Wed and Fri from 9 a.m. to 6 p.m., and Sat from 10 a.m. to 3 p.m. Limited summer hours are Mon and Thurs from 9 a.m. to 8 p.m. and Tues, Wed, and Fri from 9 a.m. to 6 p.m. Check the Web site for alternative archive hours.

History Miami

www.historymiami.org

Run by the Historical Museum of South Florida, History Miami "is the premier cultural institution committed to gathering, organizing, preserving, and celebrating Miami's history." Exhibitions, city tours, education, research, collections, and publications are available, and it's an ideal spot to find out about new archives available.

UNIVERSITY LIBRARIES

Always free for affiliates including students and professors, many libraries at local colleges and universities open their doors to the public as well. Here are a few major campus libraries around the city.

Monsignor William Barry Memorial Library

Barry University
11300 NE 2nd Ave., Miami Shores
(305) 899-3760 or (800) 756-6000, ext. 3760
www.barry.edu

Hours vary throughout the year but are typically the following during the school year: 10 a.m. to midnight on Sun, 7:30 a.m. to midnight from Mon to Thurs, 7:30 a.m. to 10 p.m. on Fri, and 9 a.m. to 10 p.m. on Sat.

College of Business and Technology

Hialeah Campus
935 West 49th St., Hialeah
(305) 273-4499, ext. 310
www.cbt.edu

Most locations are open daily from 9 a.m. to 9 p.m. Three additional libraries are at the Cutler Bay Campus, 19151 South Dixie Hwy., SW Miami (305-273-4499, ext. 400); the West Kendall Campus, 8765 SW 165th Ave., West Kendall (305-273-4499, ext. 500); and 8991 SW 107th Ave., Kendall (305-273-4499, ext. 100.)

Florida International University Libraries
Biscayne Bay Campus Library
3000 NE 151st St., North Miami
(305) 919-5718
www.fiu.edu

Library hours are typically Mon through Thurs from 7:30 a.m. to 1 a.m., Fri from 7:30 a.m. to 10 p.m., Sat from 8 a.m. to 8 p.m., and Sun from 10 a.m. to 1 a.m. A second option is the Green Library on the Modesto A. Maidique Campus, 11200 SW 8th St. (305-348-2451).

ITT Technical Institute
7955 NW 12th St., Suite 119, NW Miami
(305) 477-3080
http://itt-tech.edu

There are a number of campuses throughout the country, but this is the only one in Miami. The programs are generally distance education, so their online library system is available to the public.

Johnson and Wales University
North Miami Campus Library
1701 NE 127th St., North Miami
(305) 892-7043
http://library.jwu.edu/florida

Hours during the regular school year are Mon to Thurs from 8 a.m. to 9 p.m., Fri from 9 a.m. to 4 p.m., Sat from 10 a.m. to 5 p.m., and Sun from noon to 8 p.m. Call for more information about summer and holiday hours.

Miami Dade College Libraries
Wolfson Campus Library
300 NE 2nd Ave. Building 1
Room 1216, Downtown Miami
(305) 237-3144
www.mdc.edu

Hours are typically 8 a.m. to 9 p.m. Mon through Thurs, until 4:30 p.m. on Fri, and vary by location on Sat. Most locations are closed Sun. Check the school's Web site for other campus library information.

Miami International University of Art and Design

1501 Biscayne Blvd., Suite 100, Downtown Miami
(800) 225-9023
www.artinstitutes.edu
This academic institution offers a wide range of areas of study, including fashion design, culinary arts, and animation, to name a few.

Saint Thomas University

16401 NW 37th Ave., Miami Gardens
(305) 623-2330
www.stu.edu

This law school library is typically open Mon through Thurs from 7:30 a.m. to midnight, Fri from 7:30 a.m. to midnight, Sat from 9 a.m. to 8 p.m., and Sun from 10 a.m. to midnight.

Talmudic College of Florida

4000 Alton Rd., Miami Beach
(305) 534-7050
www.talmudicu.edu

An online and searchable library database is open to the public 24 hours a day throughout the week.

University of Miami

1300 Memorial Dr. at the Otto G. Richter Library
(305) 284-3233
www.miami.edu

With the exception of the Rosenstiel School of Marine & Atmospheric Science Library (4600 Rickenbacker Causeway, Key Biscayne; 305-421-4060), all locations are in Coral Gables and also include a music and reference library. Check the Web site for details.

HAIR, BEAUTY, & MASSAGE:
FREE STYLE

"There is only one cure for gray hair. It was invented by a Frenchman. It is called the guillotine."

—ENGLISH WRITER SIR PELHAM GRENVILLE WODEHOUSE

Who doesn't love free beauty treatments? You will find plenty of over-priced crap in this city, but if you have a little patience you're also likely to look great for very little.

FREE **SAMPLES**

Free samples are easy to come by—especially if the salesperson thinks you'll eventually buy something. Various giant malls including Dadeland and Aventura have the giant, generic beauty departments in which you can work this angle. Otherwise, here are a few spots that you're guaranteed to leave with a few sample items.

Lush
Macy's at Dadeland Mall
7303 SW 88th St., Kendall
(305) 668-1774
www.lushusa.com
This store boasts handmade bath and body products. One of their signature items is the raw soap, of which salespeople will usually let you take a sliver home with you to try. A second location is at Macy's, 1777 West 49th St., Hialeah (305-819-5870).

Sephora
721 Collins Ave., Miami Beach
(305) 532-0904
www.sephora.com

This national chain offers three free samples with every online order, and the stores typically give samples away freely as well. Check the Web site for other store locations and hours.

SCHOOL **SPECIALS**

I have firsthand experience with services like this, and I only have positive things to say. In fact, I felt more comfortable not only because of the huge price cut, but because students are constantly supervised and while they are doing the bulk of the work, their teachers are overseeing the process and making suggestions and corrections as necessary. If anything, I felt my haircuts were *more* thorough and precise. Schools are where you'll find deep discounts that are very much worth it.

Acupuncture and Massage College
10506 North Kendall Dr., Kendall
(305) 595-9500
www.amcollege.edu

Low-cost clinics are offered throughout the week by student interns and include acupuncture, cupping, and massage therapy.

Aveda Institutes
4186 South University Dr., Davie
(877) AVEDA-FL or (954) 990-0484
www.avedaflorida.com

It's a little north of Miami, but the trek is worth it. Aveda is serious about their stuff and at these prices, a few extra gas miles are justifiable. The menu includes services by Institute students and Masters, which are less and more pricey respectively— a haircut and simple style costs $12 or $18. Color retouching starts at $30 and massages start at $40. Unheard of! There are deep discounts on manicures and facials, too. Call in advance for appointments. The facility is open Mon through Fri from 9 a.m. to 8 p.m. and Sat from 8:30 a.m. to 5 p.m.

Beauty Schools of America
1176 SW 67th Ave., West Miami
(305) 267-6604
www.bsa.edu

A few sample services include $10 manicures, haircuts starting at $8, and color services starting at $22. Also, senior citizens get even deeper discounts off these prices so break out your AARP card if you have one. Call in advance for appointments. Other locations are at 1813 NE 163rd St., North Miami Beach, (305-947-0832) and 600 NE 22nd Terrace, Homestead (305-231-2302).

Educating Hands School of Massage
120 SW 8th St., Brickell area
(305) 285-6991, ext. 109
www.educatinghands.com

Student clinic massages are only $35 and available Wed at 4, 5:15, and 6:30 p.m. and Sat at 10 a.m., 11:15 a.m., and 12:30 p.m. Call in advance to make appointments.

Miami Spa Month

It is basically a restaurant week for spa treatments so if you're going to hold off to pamper yourself, wait until this event, which is typically in July each year. Past deals have included: 70-minute spa manicure and pedicure with skin exfoliation for $80 at the Biltmore Spa, a pair of 25-minute treatments from a list of eight for $100 at the Ritz-Carlton Spa in Key Biscayne, and various discounts at the best spas in town. Check www.miamispamonth.com for discounts and booking details.

Florida College of Natural Health

7925 NW 12th St., Suite 201, West Miami
(305) 597-9599
www.fcnh.com

Student therapists give 50-minute full body massages for only $25. One-hour European facials, including cleansing and exfoliation, are $30. They'll throw in an arm and hand massage. Other services, including waxing, are offered at deep discounts. Massage clinics are open Sat from 9 a.m. to 5:30 p.m. but call for an appointment for that and skin care treatments, which are offered throughout the week.

Sassoon

660 Collins Ave., Miami Beach
(305) 535-0030
www.sassoon.com

The Catch: Models, their term for volunteers who are getting free cuts, must be between 18 and 50 years old and have time and patience.

This is a "Cut and Color" position, which means that in exchange for a free cut you must have time; appointments can last up to three hours for a cut and five hours for color. Call in advance to inquire about openings and schedules.

MASSAGE **SPECIALS**

Massage Envy

13605 South Dixie Hwy. at The Falls, Kendall
(786) 430-4100
www.massageenvy.com

This cannot be beat: Your first visit is only $39 for a 50-minute massage. There are even more locations around the city so there's no excuse not to take advantage of this absurd offer. Call for schedules and appointments. Other locations are at 6927 Red Rd., South Miami (305-662-2622); 13660 SW 88th St., Kendall (305-383-1984); 256 Miracle Mile, Coral Gables (305-774-0000); and 20633 Biscayne Blvd., Aventura (305-935-1771).

The Massage Room
940 Lincoln Rd., Suite 206, Miami Beach
(786) 252-6211
http://massagebyserena.com

This is a private, licensed business run by massage school graduate Serena. Massages start at $85 for 60 minutes; mention Yelp and get a $20 discount for the first visit. Call for an appointment.

HEALTH & MEDICINE:
GOOD FOR WHAT AILS YOU

*"Be careful about reading health books.
You may die of a misprint."*

—*MARK TWAIN*

For most books, this quote is true. And perhaps it also applies to this section in many ways. This tip might be the exception: I don't know about you, but I'd rather wait in a busy waiting room for an hour and get tested for free than likely sit in a waiting room for an hour and pay to get tested, no?

With any health services, the most important thing to do is be aware and read the fine print. Consult with your regular doctor (or even lawyer!) if you have questions about papers you must sign for any treatment.

CLINICAL **STUDIES**

Clinical studies are just that: studies. Who is being studied? YOU! The benefit of participating is getting free care, drugs, treatment, and sometimes even a stipend. The catch is that these studies are conducted to help determine if certain drugs or treatments are safe to release to the public and pharmaceutical companies. Because of the nature of this delicate matter, expect abundant paperwork, ask a lot of questions, and consult with your doctor if necessary. Below are a few companies that actively seek participants and volunteers for these types of studies.

Aurora Clinical Trials
7000 SW 62nd Ave., Suite 520, South Miami
www.auroraclinicaltrials.com

Aurora runs different trials throughout the year, which are typically listed on their Web site. E-mail volunteers@auroratrials.com or check the Web site to see if you qualify.

Miami Research Associates
6141 Sunset Dr., Suite 301, South Miami
(305) 598-3125
www.miamiresearch.com

Current studies are listed on their Web site and a screening form can be filled out to determine eligibility.

National Institutes of Health
www.clinicaltrials.gov

This is probably the best first stop, as its government affiliation might make you feel a bit more at ease. The site lists various current studies by state and the contact details for interested parties.

Next Phase Clinical Trials
1900 Coral Way, Suite 200, Coral Gables
(305) 858-4300
www.nextphaseresearch.com

The Web site does not list current studies, so call or fill out the online form to find out. Otherwise, their Web site encourages visitors and e-mails to nextphase@bellsouth.net.

Suncoast Research Group
330 SW 27th Ave., Suite 506, Little Havana
(305) 631-6704
www.suncoastresearch.com

Osteoporosis, hypertension, and diabetes are a few recent studies the office has conducted. Fill out the online screening form to see if you quality for an upcoming study. A second location is at 2750 West 68th St., Suite 224, Hialeah (786-264-6677).

University of Miami School of Medicine Clinical Research Center
(305) 243-5012
www.miami.edu

The University of Miami has a clinical center dedicated to trials. Contact them via phone for information on current trials.

FREE **TESTING** & **CLINICS**

The Web site **www.freestdtestingresource.com** is a great place to start. The site lists facilities by state but doesn't include phone numbers, which presumably means you should just show up. Below are a few other testing sites that are local and confidential for STDs, pregnancy, and other conditions. Also call your local hospital for information about current clinics.

Care Resource
3510 Biscayne Blvd., Suite 300, Downtown Miami
(305) 576-1234

Free and confidential HIV testing is available from 9:30 a.m. to 5 p.m.

Eve Medical Centers
3900 NW 79th Ave., Suite 575, Doral
(305) 591-2288
www.eveabortioncarespecialists.com

Eve Medical Centers offer free pregnancy testing at both of their facilities, through blood samples and ultrasounds, if necessary. A second location is in Kendall at 8603 South Dixie Hwy. at Kendall 1 Plaza, Suite 102 (305-670-9797).

Health Council of South Florida, Inc.
8095 NW 12th St., Suite 300, Doral
(305) 592-1452, ext. 120

The Catch: The listed location is the headquarters, but not necessarily the site of clinics or events so call for details.

This organization offers free clinics and health events throughout the year. Call or e-mail manie@healthcouncil.org for details.

Miami Dade County Health Department
West Perrine Center
18255 Homestead Ave., Homestead
(305) 324-2400
www.dadehealth.org

One of the greatest perks is the free vaccines offered for children up to 18 years old. Other free testing and clinics are offered throughout the year; check the Web site for details. Other facilities are located at the Jefferson Reaves Senior Health Center, 1009 NW 5th Ave., Overtown; and at the Little Haiti Health Center, 300 NE 80th Terrace, NE Miami.

PETS:
CANINE, FELINE, BOTTOM LINE

"People are more violently opposed to fur than leather because it's safer to harass rich women than motorcycle gangs."

—ENGLISH COMEDIAN ALEXEI SAYLE

"Leopard gecko in need of a new home" was the first Miami pet classified listing I saw on the Miami page of Craigslist. It was a pretty good deal; 60 bucks for the animal, which may or may not be real, and its tank, feeding bowls, and food. Craigslist is one option for finding a new best friend, but there are others.

GET A PET

Classifieds
Check the classifieds in your local paper (see Appendix C) for ads.

Craigslist
www.craigslist.org

Buyers beware and enter at your own risk. Yes, these deals can be legit, but there's never a guarantee. Make sure your deal is not shady and most important, that no animals are being harmed in the process.

Humane Society Miami
Soffer and Fine Adoption Center
16101 West Dixie Hwy., North Miami Beach
(305) 696-0800
www.humanesocietymiami.org/petadoption.htm

These two adoption sites—a second location is in South Dade at the South Clinic at Cutler Bay, 10700 SW 211 St. (305-696-0800)—have different days and hours throughout the week, so check the Web site for details. Though adoption fees can run up to $185 for dogs, that includes spaying or neutering, a microchip and registration, one bag of Purina food, a training video, and an engraved ID tag with the pet's name and new phone number. Cat adoptions are cheaper, a maximum of $75, which includes up-to-date vaccinations, spaying or neutering, a microchip and registration, one bag of Purina food, and a training video. Plus, if you adopt a second cat it's only $10 extra!

Miami Dade Animal Services
7401 NW 74th St.
Dial 311
www.miamidade.gov/animals

The city's adoption shelter is open from 10 a.m. to 7 p.m. Mon through Fri and from 8 a.m. to 5 p.m. on Sat and Sun.

FREE **FIX:** SPAY **&** NEUTER

Miami Dade Animal Services
(305) 696-0800
www.miamidade.gov/animals/

The city's Animal Services division offers subsidized spay and neuter services for both dogs and cats. Dogs cost $30 and can be serviced on Tues. Cats cost $15 and are serviced year-round in the Miami Meow Mobile, which is a traveling Spay and Neuter Van. Call for monthly schedules.

The Cat Network, Inc.
(305) 255-3482
www.thecatnetwork.org

The Catch: You must be a member to take advantage of this service. Fortunately, membership only costs $25 per year.

You don't actually go to this place to get the spay and neuter service, but you do purchase a $25 certificate that's valid for six months at various facilities around the city.

Miami Dade Police Dept Animal Services Unit
7401 NW 74th St.
(305) 884-1101 ext 249

The police department offers low cost or free spay or neuter for all pets of county residents. Services are available at a clinic, at a travelling clinic, and at participating vets.

OTHER **CHEAP** SERVICES

Bay Road Animal Clinic
1730 Bay Rd., Miami Beach
(305) 672-2287
www.southbeachpetdoctors.com

The Catch: This deal is for first time visitors only.

This clinic offers 50 percent off a first visit with one animal. This includes a physical exam covering ears, heart, lungs, temperature, and a consultation with the doctor. Call for an appointment. The office hours are Mon through Thurs from 9 a.m. to 5 p.m., Fri from 9 a.m. to 3 p.m., and Sat from 9 a.m. to noon.

DOG **FRIENDLY** PARKS

Acadia Park
5351 NW 195th Dr., NW Miami
(305) 622-2594

Doggone Fun

There are over a dozen dog parks in the city; **Dog Friendly Parks** for leashed dogs only, **Dog Parks** for free roaming dogs, and **Dog Run Parks** for leashed dogs also. Of course, picking up after your dog and making sure their registration and vaccination information is up to date is a must. Information on all parks can be found on the county's Web site, www.miamidade.gov. Most parks are open sunrise to sunset.

Biscayne Shores and Gardens Park
11525 NE 14th Ave., Downtown Miami
(305) 654-1169

Deerwood Bonita Lakes Park
14445 SW 122nd Ave., Kendall
(305) 271-3853

Kevin Broils Park
26150 SW 125th Ave., Kendall
(305) 233-3150

Kings Meadow Park
10036 SW 142nd Ave., Kendall
(305) 380-6917

Military Trail Park
825 NE 89th St., NE Miami

Northeast Regional Dog Park at East Greynolds Park
16700 Biscayne Blvd., North Miami
(305) 945-3425

Olympic Park
8601 SW 152nd Ave., SW Miami
(305) 385-4750

Rockdale Park
9325 SW 146th St., Kendall
(786) 315-5252

San Jacinto Park
4430 SW 15th Terrace, SW Miami
(305) 666-5883

Snapper Creek Park
10280 SW 80th St., Pinecrest
(305) 666-5883

Spanish Lake Park
19405 NW 82nd Ave., NW Miami
(305) 823-2414

Tamiami Trail Park
12760 SW 6th St., SW Miami
(305) 207-2420

Tropical Park
7900 SW 40th St., Miami
(305) 226-8316

West Kendale Lakes Park
6400 Kendale Lakes Dr., Kendall
(305) 388-4771

SHOPPING:
IF YOU MUST

*"I base most of my fashion sense
on what doesn't itch."*

—*GILDA RADNER*

Almost every piece of clothing I own is from Urban Outfitters, so I never quite fit in when it came to the essence of Miami's style. There is something for everyone in the city, though; malls galore, flea markets, and consignment to get rid of your outdated trash that might be someone else's treasure.

CONSIGNMENT

Consignment stores are a great place to shop and attempt to make money off your clothes that are either out of style or no longer fit you, for better or worse. Here's a list of a few consignment stores in the city where you may find success in the form of bargains or money. Keep in mind that most of these stores take a percentage off sales and price your items themselves, so make sure you know how your items are being priced and how much the store will keep before you commit.

Baby Posh Garage
18060 West Dixie Hwy., Aventura
(305) 932-9655
www.babyposhgarage.com

This consignment store specializes in children's stuff from ages 0 to 7, with a teen extension store to boot. They typically give the customer 50% of the selling price and offer a free pickup service for a lower commission.

The Children's Exchange
1415 Sunset Dr., Coral Gables
(305) 666-6235
www.thechildrenexchange.com

My parents used to tell me they'd send me here when I misbehaved as a child! With the exception of items like undergarments and stuffed animals, this consignment store accepts an array of children's toys, clothes, and furniture. One shopping bag per consignor every two weeks is their current limit. If items don't sell in 90 days, they will be marked half off for two weeks. Profits from sold items can be collected by check or via store credit.

C Madeline's

For cheap bastards, this is more likely your stop after inheriting your grandmother's outdated collection of designer garb and not so much a place you'll be able to afford anything. Either way, if you're into classic clothing or playing dress up, this is a potentially incredible way to spend an afternoon. (Then go to Loehmann's nearby and buy stuff you can afford.) C Madeline's has been written up in *Vogue* and is internationally recognized as a leader in name brand designer vintage garb. The North Miami location is at 13702 Biscayne Blvd. and is open Mon through Sat from 11 a.m. to 6 p.m. and Sun from noon to 6 p.m. You can reach them at (305) 945-7770.

Consign of the Times
1635 Jefferson Ave., Miami Beach
(305) 535-0811
www.consignofthetimes.com

You'll get 45 percent of the selling price and the store will keep your stuff on the rack for 90 days.

The Consignment Bar
7418 Biscayne Blvd., NE Miami
(305) 751-9996
http://consignmentbar.com

This spot specializes in designer clothes and the like, and consignors can drop items off anytime from 11 a.m. to 6 p.m. on Tues through Fri. Appointments are necessary on Mon and otherwise, you can e-mail item photos to sales@consignmentbar.com to get an estimate of its retail price. They split 50/50 on all items except Chanel and Hermes handbags, which are 60/40. Items can stay in the store up to 90 days and either be returned or reduced after that.

The Fashionista Consignment Boutique

3135 Commodore Plaza, Coconut Grove
(305) 443-4331
www.thefashionistaboutique.com

The profits of sold items will be split 50/50 for items sold within 90 days. Otherwise, you can pick items up if they aren't sold.

FLEAS **NOT** INCLUDED

7th Avenue Flea Market

14135 NW 7th Ave., NW Miami

This market is known for a big jewelry selection but also has a variety of vendors on-site. It's open Thurs through Sun.

183rd Street Flea Market

18200 NW 27th Ave., NW Miami
(305) 624-1756

There's a huge selection at this market with over 400 booths and a variety of vendors. The facility is open Wed and Sun from 10 a.m. to 7 p.m. and Thurs, Fri, and Sat from 10 a.m. to 6 p.m.

Garage Sale Sources

The hands down best garage sale source is the good ol' newspaper. The *Miami Herald* lists the daily sales; typically weekend mornings are when the best ones occur. A few neighborhoods where you're bound to find treasure more than trash: Pinecrest, Aventura, Bal Harbour, and Bay Harbor.

Big Lots
8265 West Flagler St., West Miami
(305) 264-2368
www.biglots.com

There are over a dozen of these stores within 50 miles of Miami. A few are listed here that fall within Miami proper. While not explicitly a flea market, this is a great one-stop shop for cheap . . . well, everything! Hours are typically 9 a.m. to 9 p.m. daily and some stores offer delivery services. Additional locations are at 2100 SW 27th Ave., Coconut Grove (305-444-4505); 441 NE 81st St., El Portal (305-757-2909); and 11247 SW 40th St., SW Miami (305-229-7353).

Jai Alai Flea Market
3500 NW 37th Ave., Miami

On Sun, this sports venue becomes a flea market from 9 a.m. to 5 p.m. and has over 200 dealers of all types.

Swap Miami
297 NW 23rd St. at Cafeina, Miami
www.swapmiami.com

It only occurs once a year in May, but this is basically a free flea market. The swap includes clothing and home items, including furniture. Tickets are $8 in advance online or $10 at the door.

Swap Shop
3291 West Sunrise Blvd., Fort Lauderdale

If you're a Miami resident, you'll know this place by its catchy-slash-annoying radio commercials. While it's north of Miami, the drive is totally worth it. Open every day of the year, this massive place houses a flea market, movie theater, and (you guessed it!) swap shops. Open Thurs, Sat, and Sun from 7:30 a.m. to 6 p.m., Mon through Wed from 9 a.m. to 5 p.m., and Fri from 9 a.m. to 6 p.m. Admission to the space is free.

US 1 Discount Mall
18901 South Dixie Hwy., Cutler Bay
(305) 234-2828

I didn't say it's classy, but with over 200 booths at this discount flea market, you're bound to find something you think you need.

Worlds Largest Indoor Flea Market
(305) 651-9530

Held four times per year at the Miami Beach Convention Center, this flea market does have a small entrance fee of $3.50, but it's worth it.

KNICK-**KNACKS**

An overwhelming mall is not always the solution. Here are some one-stop shops for gifts and knick-knacks.

Bagua
4736 NE 2nd Ave., Downtown Miami
(305) 757-9857
http://bagua9.com

If you're looking for a funky gift boutique that also has classes, you've found it. Expect lots of Buddha-friendly knick knacks and classes including meditation and yoga.

Cheap Bastards in (Cyber) Space

A few resources for online scavenging are Craigslist (www.cragslist .org) and Freecycle (freecycle.com.) There are deals to be had on Craigslist, but first check the "free" category under "for sale."

Española Way
Miami Beach

This Miami Beach street is a favorite for boutique shopping. Clothing stores, tapas restaurants, and no shortage of unique and handmade souvenirs make this street ideal for gifts and spending an afternoon.

Five Sisters
8805 SW 132nd St., Kendall
(786) 250-4170
www.fivesisters.biz

Five Sisters has a funky hippie vibe and features cards, jewelry, and other unique gift items. Tarot readings, meditation, Reiki, and yoga classes are also offered, which range from free to private pricey sessions. Check the Web site for details.

Gift Chixx
8245 SW 124th St., Pinecrest
(305) 232-3214
http://giftchixx.com

At this more upscale boutique shop, you'll find napkin holders and Vera Bradley-esque items. The homey, family-run business makes shopping fun. Ask them about personalizing almost anything in the store.

Imagine Gifts
3252 NE 1st Ave., Downtown Miami
(305) 704-8246

"Eco-friendly," "all natural," and "recycles" are a few key words of this shop, which reflects in their merchandise selection as well. Recycled newspaper bags, funky tees, and moisturizing candles are among the ample options.

Malls with Florida Flavor

There's no shortage of strip malls and giant generic malls in Miami, but there are also quite a few stunning outdoor venues that offer year-round window-shopping and the perk of being in a city that is warm all year-round.

Bal Harbour Shops

9700 Collins Ave., Bal Harbour

www.balharbourshops.com

The Catch: Parking isn't cheap, so plan to carpool.

This is the swanky mall at which you'll likely only window-shop, unless there is a *very* big sale. Neiman Marcus trunk shows take place periodically and are listed on the Web site.

Bayside Marketplace

401 Biscayne Blvd., Downtown Miami

(305) 577-3344

www.baysidemarketplace.com

Situated on the water, this outdoor shopping space features favorites including Gap and Victoria's Secret, but also has plenty of funky boutiques and restaurants that allow for a day trip.

Cocowalk

3015 Grand Ave., Coconut Grove

(305) 444-0777

www.cocowalk.net

You'll find chains like Gap and Victoria's Secret, but there are also a bunch of cute local shops. Plus, it's one of the most gorgeous outdoor places to stroll around for shopping, food, people-watching, and nightlife. Nightclubs open until 3 a.m.

The Falls

8888 SW 136th St., Kendall

(305) 255-4570

www.simon.com

You'll find all your favorites here including Gap, Bloomingdales, Macy's, and other basics; Coach, BCBG, Abercrombie, and others. It's outdoors and has several restaurants with outdoor seating. Plus, there's a movie theater if you want to hibernate.

Lincoln Road

Lincoln Road between Collins Avenue and Bay Road, Miami Beach
www.lincolnroad.org
This outdoor walking mall is prime real estate for people-watching and shopping alike. You'll find basics like American Apparel, Gap, and Steve Madden, but you'll also come across some hidden gems and funky boutiques. Also check into farmers' markets and festivals that set up on the street.

Sunset Place

5701 Sunset Dr., Suite 350, South Miami
(305) 663-0873
www.simon.com
This is another great local place for outdoor shopping with favorites including Urban Outfitters, Lucky Brand, and Banana Republic, among others. There is also a movie theater, and IMAX 3-D theater for special shows.

Village of Merrick Park

358 San Lorenzo Ave., Coral Gables
(305) 448-0098
www.villageofmerickpark.com
The Catch: Parking isn't cheap, but it will be if you get your ticket stamped in Nordstrom, which they'll typically do whether or not you make a purchase.
Merrick Park is a fairly new development in the heart of Coral Gables. It's a fancy spot that'll yield window shopping, mostly, but also offers beautiful strolling space. Check the Web site for events that feature live music and sales.

OUTLET & WHOLESALE SHOPPING

If outlets are your thing, these malls will be your new best friends. If possible, go on weekdays. If weekends are your only option, remember this: they are everyone else's only option, too.

Dolphin Mall
11401 NW 12th Street, NW Miami
(305) 591-1877
www.shopdolphinmall.com
Hours: Mon through Sat from 10 a.m. to 9:30 p.m.; Sun from 11 a.m. to 7 p.m.

A few of the outlets you shouldn't miss include Saks Fifth Avenue Off 5th, Banana Republic Factory Store, Bloomingdale's the Outlet Store, Gap Outlet, and the Neiman Marcus Last Call Clearance Center, among others.

Miami International Merchandise Mart
777 NW 72nd Ave., NW Miami
(305) 261-2900
http://doubletree1.hilton.com

The Catch: Call a store in advance; sometimes getting in requires an "appointment."

Always wanted wholesale discounts but didn't want to buy in bulk? The Mart is the place for regular shoppers who want deep discounts, mostly on jewelry, and sometimes on clothing that isn't too tacky.

Prime Outlets
250 East Palm Dr., Florida City
.(305) 248-4736
www.primeoutlets.com
Hours: Mon through Sat from 10 a.m. to 9 p.m.; Sun from 11 a.m. to 6 p.m.; closed on major holidays

This one is probably closer to Key Largo than Miami, but it's worth the drive for certain outlets including the Barney's New York Outlet, BCBG Max Azria Factory Store, Nike Factory Store, and others.

Sawgrass Mills Mall

12801 West Sunrise Blvd., Sunrise
(954) 846-2350
www.simon.com
Hours: Mon through Sat from 10 a.m. to 9:30 p.m.; Sun from 11 a.m. to 8
p.m.

It's not technically in Miami, but it's worth the drive if you're in the northern part of the city. Outlets include a Barney's New York Outlet, Burlington Coat Factory, Calvin Klein Company Store, and Neiman Marcus Last Call Clearance Center, among dozens of others.

THRIFT **SHOPS**

Salvation Army and Goodwill are two standard national chains, but there are some other locals that might yield some trash and treasure.

Antique and Collectibles Market

Coconut Grove MayFair Market, Coconut Grove
Lincoln Road Mall Market, Miami Beach
(305) 673-4991

This outdoor thrift shopping extravaganza takes place about five times per year in each location and typically happens on different weekends at each location. It's always free to the public but parking might be a challenge. Expect an excellent selection of thrifty clothes, jewelry, and knick-knacks.

Fly Boutique

650 Lincoln Rd., Miami Beach
(305) 604-8508
http://flyboutiquevintage.com

This is a Lincoln Road favorite, especially among chains that are infiltrating the once-quirky street. The merchandise is often overpriced, but with some sifting, it is possible to find an affordable gem.

Miami Twice
6562 Bird Rd., South Miami area
(305) 666-0127
http://miamitwice.com

Check out thrifty deals at this well-known Bird Road store and play dress up with the designer garb that's probably too pricey for the average cheap bastard.

Red, White and Blue Thrift Store
901 East 10th Ave., Suite 12, Hialeah
(305) 887-5351

This place is so much more than a thrift store. In fact, plan to dedicate an entire day to their racks. They're open Mon through Sat from 9 a.m. to 6 p.m.

Exploring Miami

ACCOMMODATIONS:
CHEAP HOSPITALITY

"'Do Not Disturb' signs should be written in the language of the hotel maids."

—AMERICAN COMEDIAN TIM BEDORE

Thought hostels were portrayed accurately in that that scary Eli Roth movie or were reserved for European backpacking trips? Think again. There are a slew of them in Miami Beach, especially, and they are worth the downgrade for penny pinchers on a budget. How much time will you really be spending in your room, anyway?

CHEAP **HOSTELS** & HOTELS

Chateau Bleau Hotel
1111 Ponce de Leon Blvd., Coral Gables
(305) 448-2634
http://hotelchateaubleau.com

Among the only true budget accommodations in Coral Gables, this hotel has rates starting around $24 per bed per night for a four-bed dorm room. Rooms with double beds cost around $45 per person per night. There's 24-hour reception and free transfers to and from Miami International Airport and the Port of Miami.

The Clay Hotel
1438 Washington Ave., Miami Beach
(800) 379-CLAY (2529)
www.clayhotel.com

The Catch: Private rooms do not include bathrooms, but it's still a sweet deal for two people.

A private room with a double bed starts at $60 per night, which is not bad compared to what you'll find hotel-wise in this neighborhood. For a bit less, grab a solo bed starting at $20 per night.

Deco Walk Hostel
928 Ocean Dr., Second Floor, Miami Beach
(305) 531-5511
www.decowalkhostel.com

It's the only hostel on Ocean Drive and has glowing ratings all around. Free perks include a daily breakfast from 8 to 10 a.m. daily, linens and towels, free Wi-Fi, secure luggage storage and bike parking, kitchen access, and 24-hour security and reception, among others. Rates start at $25 per bed for a 10-person dorm and go up to $29 for a six-bed female-only dorm.

The Greenview Hotel
1671 Washington Ave., Miami Beach
(305) 531-6588
www.greenviewhotel.com

This spectacular location can't be beat, especially for a hotel with rates like this. Room rates start at $49.50 per person per night for a room with a double bed and $99 for a one-person room. Amenities include free Internet access and cable TV in all rooms.

Havana Hostel
619 SW 6th St., Little Havana
www.hostelmiami.com

The Catch: This spot requires a four-night minimum stay, but the fifth night is free with that.

Don't expect South Beach, but do expect another historic neighborhood if you're looking for something off the beaten path. In the heart of Little Havana, you'll have access to some of the most delicious Latin food in town and can access Miami Beach via a nearby bus line that runs 24 hours per day. Prices are about $35 per night per person.

Island House South Beach
1428 Collins Ave., Miami Beach
(800) 382-2422 or (305) 864-2422
www.islandhousesouthbeach.com

The Catch: Room rates vary per season. Summer is May 1 through November 21; winter is November 22 through April 30.

A full breakfast buffet and free happy hour beer are two big perks. The rates are another: Summer rates for junior rooms, with double or queen beds, start at $79; the same rooms are $89 in the winter.

Jazz on South Beach

321 Collins Ave., Miami Beach
(305) 672-2137
www.jazzhostels.com

Located between 3rd and 4th streets on Collins Avenue, rates fluctuate throughout the year, but a stay always includes the following free perks: Wi-Fi in common areas, breakfast, linens and towels, luggage storage, and touristy maps and literature. Average rates are $24 per bed in a 4-bed dorm, $20 per bed in an 8-bed dorm, $17 in a 12-bed dorm, and $75 for a private room with a queen-size bed.

Miami Beach International Travellers Hostel

236 9th St., Miami Beach
(305) 534-0268
www.hostelmiamibeach.com

For prices that start at $27 a night and free breakfast, lunch, and dinner (according to the Web site), you would certainly save a lot of money for alcohol! Other incentives include a pretty sweet location, free Wi-Fi, towels, linens, and the occasional free drink at the music and dance parties. Lockers are available and 24-hour reception and security is a plus.

Motel Blu Miami

7700 Biscayne Blvd., NE Miami
(305) 757-8451
www.motelblu.com

If you're looking for a spot in this hood, you'll find a ton of amenities include shuttle service to and from the airport and cruise port, individual AC control, free wireless, free parking, and light breakfast. Rates start as low as $20 per person for a two-person room with single beds.

Red Roof Inn
3401 NW LeJeune Rd. at Miami International Airport, NW Miami
(305) 871-4221
www.redroof.com

This ain't the Ritz, but it's a great crash pad for early airport departures. Rates start at $70.99 per night for rooms with two full beds and free Wi-Fi.

South Beach Hostel
235 Washington Ave., Miami Beach
(305) 534-6669
www.southbeachhostel.com

The Catch: They only allow guests 18 and older.

Beds start at $17.95 per night and free breakfast and Wi-Fi are always included. A huge plus is their free airport transportation from Miami International. This spot is also secure with keys for every room (including bathrooms) and a 24-hour reception desk. Most importantly, their claim to fame: "Miami Beach's only full liquor hostel bar." It's open until 5 a.m. daily and serves $1.50 beer during happy hour daily from 6 to 8 p.m.

Tropics Hotel and Hostel
1550 Collins Ave., Miami Beach
(305) 531-0361
www.tropicshotel.com

The Catch: Rates vary seasonally (i.e. beds that are $34 around spring break and New Year's go for $20 during off-season)

A four-person room at $30 per person per night is a deal, but singles and cheapies can take advantage of their lowest $20 per bed rates, which vary seasonally. A twin private room is about $30 to $40 per night, which typically accommodates two people.

ART GALLERIES:
SHOW ME THE MONET!

"Bad artists always admire each other's work."

—*OSCAR WILDE*

Miami might be one of the best places to take advantage of free art galleries around the city. One great resource is **Art Circuits Miami Guide** (www.artcircuits.com), which has updated comprehensive listings of art-related activities, galleries, and the like in the city by neighborhood. Below is an assortment of galleries all over the city, most of which are free to browse and hold special events throughout the year. However, I suggest checking Web sites for specific neighborhoods (see page 262) for comprehensive gallery listings.

ART **GALLERIES**

101/Exhibit
101 NE 40th St., Downtown Miami
(305) 573-2101
www.101exhibit.com

Fine and decorative art and design are highlighted at this gallery. Their mission is to "provide a dynamic program unrestricted by era, locale, or convention." Open Tues through Sat from 11 a.m. to 7 p.m.

A. Dale Nally Studio
2315 NW 2nd Ave., Downtown Miami
(305) 724-6021
www.adalenally.com

A. Dale Nally's art is exhibited in his Wynwood Gallery. His paintings have been exhibited around the country. Open during the gallery walks the second Sat of each month from 7 to 11 p.m.; by appointment daily.

Adamar Fine Arts
4141 NE 2nd Ave., Suite 107, Downtown Miami
(305) 576-1355
www.popnart.com

This gallery exhibits dozens of artists and much of the current collection can be viewed on the Web site. Open Mon through Fri from 11 a.m. to 6 p.m.; Sat by appointment.

Agustin Gainza Arts

1652 SW 8th St., Little Havana
(305) 644-5855
www.agustingainza.com

Cuban-American artist Agustin Gainza features his painting, drawing, print-making, and ceramics in this studio. Call for schedules.

Alejandra von Hartz Gallery

2630 NW 2nd Ave., Downtown Miami
(305) 438-0220
www.alejandravonhartz.net

Contemporary art is the major focus of this gallery with emphases on Latin American and minimalism. Open Tues through Fri from 11 a.m. to 6 p.m.; Sat from noon to 5 p.m.

The Americas Collection

214 Andalusia Ave., Coral Gables
(305) 446-5578
www.americascollection.com

This collection showcases contemporary Latin American art and was founded in 1991. Check the Web site for free opening events and receptions. Open Mon through Fri from 10:30 a.m. to 5:30 p.m.; Sat from noon to 5 p.m.

Art Space/Virginia Miller Galleries

169 Madeira Ave., Coral Gables
(305) 444-4493
www.virginiamiller.com

Virginia Miller opened her gallery in 1974 and now curates various exhibitions of Latin American artists. Open Mon through Fri 11 a.m. to 6 p.m.; Sat by appointment.

Art Center/South Florida

800/801 Lincoln Rd., Miami Beach
(305) 674-8278
www.artcentersf.org

These galleries provide subsidized studio space to local budding artists. It's always free and open to the public and is a great place to see innovative work. Hours vary.

Artformz Alternative

171 NW 23rd St., Downtown Miami
(305) 572-0040
www.artformz.net

Founded in 2004, this 1,300-square-foot space exhibits innovative and diverse art. Open Tues through Fri noon to 7 p.m.; Sat from noon to 5 p.m.

ARTSEEN at New World School of the Arts

2215 NW 2nd Ave., Downtown Miami
(305) 237-7007
http://artseenspace.wordpress.com

This is the exhibition space for student work from the New World School of the Arts. Open Mon through Fri from 6 to 10 p.m.

Bakehouse Art Complex

561 NW 32 St., Downtown Miami
(305) 576-2828
www.bacfl.org

See the work of various emerging contemporary artists at this space. Free opening receptions are held the second Fri of every month for new exhibitions. Open daily from noon to 5 p.m.

Barbara Gillman Gallery

2320 North Miami Ave., Downtown Miami
(305) 538-5895
www.barbaragillmangallery.com

Florida artists are the specialty at this gallery, which opened in the late 1970s. Contemporary American and Latin American art of all mediums are also featured. Open Mon through Thurs from noon to 7 p.m.; Fri and Sat from noon to 9 p.m.

Blu Moon Studio of Art

3444 Main Hwy., Coconut Grove
(305) 529-5006
www.artclassesinmiami.com

Sheri Friedman, a "magical realist" artist, offers art classes for children and adults at her Coconut Grove studio. Hours are by appointment.

Bottero Studio

17 NW 36th St., Downtown Miami
(305) 573-6303
www.botterodaniel.com

Daniel Bottero was trained in Italy, worked in Paris, and now lives in New York. His work is featured in prestigious collections including those of Senator Hillary Rodham Clinton, Gloria and Emilio Estefan, and Oscar de la Hoya. Hours are by appointment.

Britto Central

818 Lincoln Rd., Miami Beach
(305) 531-8821
www.britto.com

Roam around Miami and you'll notice quickly that Romeo Britto is a local favorite. His artwork is publicly displayed all over the city and is featured at shopping malls and in hotels alike. Stop into his Lincoln Road gallery to check out some of his latest work—both that you can and cannot afford. Open Sun through Thurs from 10 a.m. to 11 p.m.; Fri and Sat from 10 a.m. to midnight.

Calix Gustav Gallery

98 NW 29th St., Downtown Miami
(305) 576-8116
www.calixgustav.com

This visual arts studio has rotating exhibits of new and emerging artists. Open Tues through Fri from noon to 6 p.m.; Sat from noon to 5 p.m.

Carel Gallery

922 Lincoln Rd., Miami Beach
(305) 534-4384
www.carelgallery.com

This gallery specializes in modern and 19th-century art of various artists. Its mission is to make contemporary art more publically accessible. Open Mon through Sat from 10:30 a.m. to 6 p.m.

Cisneros Fontanals Art Foundation

1018 North Miami Ave., NE Miami
(305) 455-3380
www.cifo.org

The Cisneros Fontanals Art Foundation fosters "cultural exchange among the visual arts and is dedicated to the support of emerging and mid-career contemporary multidisciplinary artists from Latin America." Open Thurs through Sun from noon to 5 p.m.; by appointment.

Coconut Grove Gallery and Interiors

2884 Bird Ave., Coconut Grove
(305) 445-7401
www.coconutgrovegallery.com

This 15,000-foot showroom was opened by Midwesterners who migrated south in the mid-1980s. Today, their showroom includes an array of furniture, art, and interiors. Open Mon through Sat from 10 a.m. to 6 p.m.; extended hours on Wed until 7:30 p.m.

Collection Privée

918 Lincoln Rd., Miami Beach
(786) 276-7600
www.collectionprivee.com

This gallery highlights contemporary sculptures from artists around the world. They will assist you with tracking down pieces of interest. Open daily from 11 a.m. to 6 p.m. and 7 to 11 p.m.

Cremata Gallery

1646 SW 8 St., Little Havana
(305) 644-3315
www.crematagallery.com

According to the gallery, the work exhibited "is the product of the life experiences of two avid travelers and art collectors." Open Tues through Sat from noon to 7 p.m.

Cristina Chacon Studio Gallery

3162 Commodore Plaza, Coconut Grove
(305) 442-2884
www.cristinachaconstudiogallery.com

Contemporary fine art is what you'll find at this gallery, which represents artists from around the world. Open Tues through Fri from 11:30 a.m. to 5 p.m.; always open by appointment.

Cuba Ocho Art and Research Center

1465 SW 8th St., Suite 106–107, Little Havana
(305) 285-5880
www.cubaochoartcenter.com

For over two decades, this spot has specialized in Cuban art. Their research center includes a library that dates back to 1850. Check their Web site for art auctions and fairs. Call for schedules.

D & G Art Design Gallery

540 NW 28th St., Downtown Miami
(305) 438-9798
www.dgfineart.com

European, American, and Latin American contemporary artists are featured here. The gallery also offers appraisals, restoration, and other art services. Open Mon through Fri from 9 a.m. to 5 p.m.; private showings by appointment.

de la Cruz Collection Contemporary Art Space

23 NE 41st St., Downtown Miami
(305) 576-6112
www.delacruzcollection.org

The 30,000-square-foot space showcases the personal international contemporary art collection of Rosa and Carlos de la Cruz. Check the Web site for performances and events that take place in the space. Open Wed through Sat from 10 a.m. to 4 p.m.; Tues by appointment.

Diana Lowenstein Fine Arts

2043 North Miami Ave., Downtown Miami
(305) 576-1804
www.dlfinearts.com

Gallery owner and director Diana Lowenstein features international art in this space. Open Tues through Fri from 10 a.m. to 5 p.m.; Sat from 10 a.m. to 3 p.m.

Diaspora Vibe Art Gallery

3938 North Miami Ave. in the Madonna Building, Downtown Miami
(305) 573-4046
www.diasporavibe.net

Their mission statement includes promoting, nurturing, and cultivating "the vision and diverse talent of emerging artists from the Latin and Caribbean Diaspora through the artists in residence program, international exchanges, and community and youth activities that celebrate Miami's rich cultural and social fabric." From May through October, participate in the Final Fridays event on the last Fri of every month from 7 to 11 p.m., which includes featured art of a chosen artist as well as music, food, and other arts. Call and check the Web site for other events throughout the month. Open Tues through Fri from 11 a.m. to 6 p.m.; Sat from noon to 4 p.m. by appointment.

Dina Mitrani Gallery

2620 NW 2nd Ave., Downtown Miami
(786) 486-7248
www.dinamitranigallery.com

Photography is the focus of Mitrani's Wynwood gallery. Mitrani also participates in the local community events. Open Tues through Fri from 1 to 5 p.m.; by appointment.

Dot Fiftyone Gallery

51 NW 36 St., Downtown Miami
(305) 573-9994
www.dotfiftyone.com

A rotating variety of artists are featured here and the Web site frequently lists current shows and artist bios. Open Mon through Fri from 11 a.m. to 7:30 p.m.; Sat from 1 to 6 p.m.

Durban Segnini Gallery

3072 SW 38th Ave., Coral Gables
(305) 774-7740
www.durbansegnini.com

Founded in 1970 in Venezuela, this gallery features contemporary painting and sculpture. A second location is at 2145 NW 2nd Ave. in Downtown Miami. Open Mon through Fri from 10 a.m. to 6 p.m.

Evelyn S. Poole, Ltd. Antiques Gallery

3925 North Miami Ave., Downtown Miami
www.evelynpooleltd.com

This 5,000-square-foot gallery features "museum quality decorative 17th, 18th and 19th century and art deco furniture and accessories." Open Tues through Thurs from 10:30 a.m. to 4 p.m.

Gallery Deja Vu

631 Lincoln Road, Miami Beach
(305) 604-5993
www.gallerydejavu.com

Their collection "ranges from true antiques to contemporary art" and includes items from bronzes to furniture. Open daily from 10 a.m. to 11 p.m.

Godon America

1 NE 40th St., Suite 5, Downtown Miami
(786) 362-5546
www.godonamerica.com

This gallery features the work of French painter and sculptor Alain Godon. Open Mon through Sat from 11 a.m. to 6 p.m.

GroveHouse Artists

3390 Mary St., Suite 162
(305) 569-3097
www.grovehouseartists.net

This venue serves as a gallery for local artists to exhibit and also plays host to various events and showings. Open Mon by appointment; Tues through Thurs from noon to 6 p.m.; Fri and Sat from noon to 9 p.m.; Sun from 11 a.m. to 5 p.m.

H. Benitez Fine Art Gallery

305 Alcazar Ave. Suite 4, Coral Gables
(786) 877-1045
www.humbertobenitez.com

Humberto Benitez is a Cuban-born artist and is known for his colorful paintings. Much of his art is inspired by his homeland, which is reflected in the vibrant scenes and colors. Open Mon through Fri from 11:30 a.m. to 6 p.m.

Gallery Nights

Several areas in the city host gallery nights, in which the local establishments open their doors late and often offer food and hors d'oeuvres to the public.

Brickell Gallery Nights
www.downtownmiami.com
This event takes place on the third Thurs of every month from 7 to 9 p.m.

Coconut Grove Gallery Walk
www.coconutgrove.com
This event takes place the first Sat of every month from 7 to 10 p.m.

Gables Gallery Night
(305) 444-4493
www.coralgables.com
The first Fri of every month, galleries keep their doors open from 7 to 10 p.m. along Ponce de Leon Boulevard in Coral Gables. Take advantage of gratis art advice, transportation between galleries, and free wine and cheese.

Hardcore Art Contemporary Space
33326 North Miami Ave., Miami Gardens
(786) 488-4375
www.hardcoreartcontemporary.com

This space is over 6,000 square feet and "dedicated to contemporary projects and cutting edge artists." Open Tues through Fri from 10 a.m. to 6 p.m.; Sat from 11 a.m. to 4 p.m.

Harold Golen Gallery
2294 NW 2nd Ave., Downtown Miami
(305) 989-3359
www.haroldgolengallery.com

Gallery Walk
http://miamidesigndistrict.net
Miami's Design District, from NE 36th to NE 41st streets west of Biscayne Boulevard in Downtown Miami, has a gallery walk event on the second Sat of each month. Galleries stay open until 10 p.m. and usually offer beverages. This same event takes place in the Wynwood area downtown.

Lincoln Road & Miami Beach Art Walk
www.artcentersf.org
From 7 to 10 p.m. the first Sat of the month, over 40 local galleries, museums, and artists open their doors for this event.

NoMi Gallery Walk & MoCA Jazz
770 NE 125th St., North Miami
(305) 893-6211
www.mocanomi.org
On the last Fri of each month, the City of North Miami and the Museum of Contemporary Art team up for this event, featuring live jazz concerts at MoCA and extended viewing hours from 8 to 9:30 p.m. Take advantage of free tours available; the museum welcomes donations.

Pop-Surrealist art is shown at this gallery, which participates in the second Saturday Gallery Walk Nights. Check the Web site for openings of events of the featured artists. Open Mon through Fri from 9:30 a.m. to 5:30 p.m.; Sat from noon to 5:30 p.m.

Ideobox Art Space
2417 North Miami Ave., Downtown Miami
(305) 576-9878
www.ideobox.com

Contemporary art is the focus at this Wynwood gallery. Open daily from 10 a.m. to 5 p.m. by appointment.

Imago Art Gallery
1615 SW 8th St., Little Havana
(305) 642-1133
www.imagofineartgallery.com

This gallery shows contemporary Cuban paintings. Open Tues through Sat from noon to 7 p.m.; by appointment.

Jorge M. Sori Fine Art
2970 Ponce de Leon Blvd., Coral Gables
(305) 657-3151
http://jorgesorifineart.com

Latin American art is their specialty. Open Tues through Fri from 11 a.m. to 5:30 p.m.; Sat by appointment.

Ka.Be Contemporary
123 NW 23rd St., Downtown Miami
(305) 573-8142
www.kabecontemporary.com

This contemporary art gallery exhibits work of emerging artists from drawing and photography to painting. Open Tues through Fri from 11 a.m. to 3 p.m.; by appointment.

Kavachnina Contemporary
46 NW 36th St., Downtown Miami
(305) 448-2060
www.kavachnina.com

Recently renamed from Art Rouge, this gallery showcases the Kavachnina collection, which spans over two decades. Open Mon through Fri from 11 a.m. to 6 p.m.; Sat by appointment.

Kelley Roy Gallery
50 NE 29 St., Downtown Miami
(305) 444-0004
www.kelleyroygallery.com

Emerging artists are highlighted at this Wynwood gallery. Open Tues through Fri from 11 a.m. to 5 p.m.; by appointment.

Klara Chavarria Contemporary Art Gallery and Studio Space
2912 Ponce de Leon Blvd., Coral Gables
(305) 282-2116
www.klarachavarria.com

A Guatemalan-born contemporary artist exhibits her paintings and works in this space. Open Tues through Fri from 11 a.m. to 5 p.m.; Sat from noon to 5 p.m.; by appointment other days and times.

Lisa Remeny Studio and Gallery
(305) 854-9485
www.lisaremeny.com

Miami native Lisa Remeny has been exhibiting her tropically inspired artwork since the 1980s. She's been commissioned to create murals all over the country and has exhibited worldwide. Call or e-mail info@lisaremeny.com to schedule a viewing appointment at her Coconut Grove gallery. Hours are by appointment only.

Locust Projects
155 NE 38th St., Suite 100, Downtown Miami
(305) 576-8570
www.locustprojects.org

This gallery supports installations including photography, video, sculpture, drawing, painting, and digital media. Open Thurs through Sat from noon to 5 p.m.

Luis Perez Galería at the Awarehouse
550 NW 29th St., Downtown Miami
(305) 379-3763
www.luisperezgaleria.com

Colombian artists' work is the focus here, but various international artists show their art in the space. Call for schedules.

Lyle O. Reitzel Gallery Miami
2441 NW 2nd Ave., Downtown Miami
(786) 693-8155
www.lyleoreitzel.com

This gallery features art from the Dominican Republic, Cuba, and the Caribbean as well as other countries in Latin America and internationally. Open Wed through Fri from 10 a.m. to 6 p.m.; Sat from noon to 6 p.m.

The Margulies Collection At The Warehouse
591 NW 27th St., Downtown Miami
(305) 576-1051
www.margulieswarehouse.com

The Catch: Admission is $10 for general admission and free for students with ID.

Contemporary and vintage photography is showcased here as well as sculpture and other works. Open Wed through Sat from 11 a.m. to 4 p.m.

Mildrey Guillot Art Gallery
1654 SW 8th St., Little Havana
(305) 538-1498 or (305) 642-6122
www.mildreyguillot.com

This artist was born in Havana and trained in Spain; charcoals, pastels, and oils are the media you'll see most. Open Tues through Fri from 11 a.m. to 5 p.m.; Sat from 11 a.m. to 4 p.m.

Miriam Fernandes Gallery
3618 NE 2nd Ave., Downtown Miami
(305) 588-2912
www.miriamfernandes.com

The collection focuses on artists from Brazil and North America. Open Sat from 11 a.m. to 6 p.m.; weekdays by appointment.

Molina Fine Art Gallery & Studio
1634 SW 8th St., Little Havana
(305) 642-0444
www.molinaartgallery.com

Afro-Cuban folklore is the highlight of this gallery and studio. Open Mon through Sat from 11 a.m. to 7 p.m.; Sun by appointment.

Nina Torres Fine Art

2033 NW 1st Place, Downtown Miami
(973) 270-7774
www.ninatorresfineart.com

This is another gallery featuring Latin American artists. Open Mon through Sat from 11 a.m. to 5 p.m.

Pan American Art Projects

2450 NW 2nd Ave., Downtown Miami
(305) 573-2400
www.panamericanart.com

North and Latin American artists are typically featured at this gallery. Open Tues through Fri from 9:30 a.m. to 5:30 p.m.; Sat from noon to 5:30 p.m.

Peter Lik

701 Lincoln Rd., Miami Beach
(786) 235-9570
www.peterlik.com

Lik's fine art photography of outdoors and landscapes are featured here. Open 10 a.m. to midnight daily; appointment preferred.

RDZ Fine Art

37 Merrick Way, Coral Gables
(305) 720-5172
http://rdzfineart.com

A variety of contemporary paintings and photography is featured here. The site also plays host to events and viewings. Open Tues through Thurs from 4 to 6 p.m.; Fri from 5 to 9 p.m.; Sat from noon to 9 p.m.

RodezArt.com Gallery

3015 Grand Ave., Suite 237 in CocoWalk, Coconut Grove
(786) 543-7237
www.rodezart.com

The art of George Rodez, who lived in Cuba as a child, has been exhibited worldwide and can be viewed at this Coconut Grove gallery. Open Sun through Thurs from 11 a.m. to 7 p.m.; Fri and Sat from 11 a.m. to 10 p.m.

The Rubell Family Collection
95 NW 29th St., Downtown Miami
(305) 573-6090

Consider it more of an art museum than an art gallery. This might justify the $10 admission. Take advantage of $5 reduced admission for students and individuals under 18. Open Wed through Sat from 10 a.m. to 6 p.m.

Sammer Gallery
82 NE 29th St., Downtown Miami
(305) 441-2005
www.artnet.com/sammergallery.html

This gallery focuses on Uruguayan artists and the promotion of Constructivism.

Windisch-Hunt Fine Art
2911 Grand Ave., Coconut Grove
(772) 480-3131
http://windisch-hunt.com

Several artists at a time are featured here and collaborations are made with local organizations. Open Tues through Fri from 10 a.m. to 8 p.m.; Sat from 10 a.m. to 9 p.m.; Sat from 10 a.m. to 9 p.m.; Sun from noon to 8 p.m.

Wallflower Gallery
(305) 579-0069
www.wallflowergallery.com

The gallery moved out of its location in May 2010 and was in the process of relocating. Check the Web site for updates. Typically, they are open for events, appointments, and based on the exhibition taking place.

Zu Galeria
2248 SW 8th St., Little Havana
(786) 443-5872
www.zugaleria.com

As a new gallery in Little Havana, this space is dedicated to promoting emerging artists from around the world. Open Tues through Sat from 11 a.m. to 6 p.m.

BICYCLING:
FREE WHEELING

"Bicycles are almost as good as guitars for meeting girls."

—*BOB WEIR*

Not every inch of Miami is bike friendly (stay away from major highways!), but there are ample green space, parks, and bike-friendly neighborhoods that make biking in the city worthwhile. A variety of shops arrange hourly or daily rentals, not only of bicycles but also skates and tandems.

BIKE **RENTALS**

Bike and Roll
210 10th St., Miami Beach
(305) 604-0001
www.bikeandroll.com

Bike rentals start at $8 per hour and $25 per day. All bike rentals include locks, helmets, maps, and other accessories. Daily two-and-a-half-hour Art Deco bike tours depart at 10:30 a.m. and 2:30 p.m. The tour costs $39 for adults and $29 for students, including the bike.

Bill Baggs Cape Florida State Park
1200 South Crandon Blvd., Key Biscayne
(305) 361-5811
www.floridastateparks.org/capeflorida

The Catch: There's a parking fee that's $4 for a single occupant and $8 for two or more occupants.

Bike rentals are $3 per half hour and $5 per hour for cruiser bicycles; $5 per half hour and $8 per hour for English bikes, tandem bikes, and tricycles; and $10 per half hour and $15 per hour for quad bikes that seat four people. Even larger bikes that seat four people plus two small children are available for $15 per half hour and $25 per hour. The park itself is open from 8 a.m. to around 7 p.m. (or whenever sunset happens to be) daily and throughout the year.

Fritz's Skate, Bike and Surf Shop

1620 Washington Ave., Miami Beach
(305) 532-1954
www.fritzsmiamibeach.com

The Catch: Deposits are required, but are returnable. For bicycle rentals, it's $200, which can be given in cash or credit.

This reputable Miami Beach shop rents bicycles for $10 per hour or $24 for a 24-hour period, so you can keep the bike overnight and returned at the time of rental the following day. Consider the $70 per week option if you're in town for that long (or buy a crappier bike cheaper on Cragslist!). Roller-blades are the same prices but only require a $100 returnable deposit. All items come with a lock, key, and helmet.

JB Bike Shop

7316 Collins Ave., Miami Beach
(305) 866-3622
http://jbbikeshop.com

The Catch: Mountain bikes require a $250 refundable deposit—refundable, just be prepared to shell it out initially.

Rentals start at $24 per day for mountain bikes and go up to $45 daily for more serious road bikes. Weekly rentals are also possible.

Mangrove Cycles

260 Crandon Blvd. Suite 6, Key Biscayne
(305) 361-5555
www.mangrovecycles.com

Rentals start at $15 per two hours, but you're better off getting the $20 per day deal. Luxury and performance bikes cost a bit more, but a regular ol' thang is just fine for the flatlands of Miami.

Miami Beach Bicycle Center

601 5th St., Miami Beach
(305) 531-4161
www.bikemiamibeach.com

Hourly rentals start at $8 and daily rentals cost $24. They also carry tandem bikes for really cute couples who want to make everyone jealous.

Miami Critical Mass

On the last Friday of every month, bicyclists and other "self-pro-pelled commuters", according to the organization, gather to ride together to support these means of transportation. Check **http://miamibikescene.blogspot.com** for updates and locations. The aver-age speed is a reasonable 12 to 15 mph and participation is free. Check the Web site for a calendar of events.

Wheeleez Rentals
1655 James Ave., Miami Beach
(305) 428-2767
www.miamibicyclerentals.com

Rentals start at $9 per hour and $27 per day, which includes maps, helmets, locks, front packs, and baskets for no extra charge.

BIKE **RESOURCES**

Here are a few Web sites that cyclists can utilize:

Bike Miami Blog
http://bikemiamiblog.wordpress.com

A useful resource for events and rides in the city.

Map My Ride
www.mapmyride.com

This is an ideal resource for finding and mapping rides. Events are also listed.

Miami Bike Scene
http://miamibikescene.blogspot.com

This site lists local events and shops.

GARDENS & GARDENING:
DIRT CHEAP

"According to a survey in this week's Time *magazine, 85 percent of Americans think global warming is happening. The other 15 percent work for the White House."*

—JAY LENO

If you think beaches are overrated, there are plenty of outdoor sanctuaries that are not inundated with scantily clad beach bums. A plethora of outdoor green space in the city offers an escape from city life, as well as impressive, sometimes award-winning scenery and art for reasonable prices.

PUBLIC GARDENS

The Ancient Spanish Monastery
16711 East Dixie Hwy., North Miami Beach
(305) 945-1462
www.spanishmonastery.com
Open Mon through Sat from 10 a.m. to 4 p.m.; Sun from noon to 4 p.m.

The monastery itself, built from 1133 to 1141 A.D. in Spain, is perhaps the oldest building in the Western Hemisphere, according to the Web site. William Randolph Hearst dismantled and shipped it to the United States in 1925; since 1952 its home has been in Miami. The gardens are another draw for visitors and tours are available almost daily. Admission is $5 per person and $2.50 for seniors and students with ID.

Fairchild Tropical Botanic Garden
10901 Old Cutler Rd., Coral Gables
(305) 667-1651
www.fairchildgarden.org
Hours: Daily from 9:30 a.m. to 4:30 p.m.

This garden is well-known for its impressive grounds and art showcases. Most notably, the work of Dale Chihuly has been showcased as part of the landscape; a variety of other artists are featured throughout the year. A shuttle service is provided and the first Wed of each month is pay-what-you-wish. If you're visiting any other day, print the $5 coupon on the Web site. Admission is $20 for adults, $15 for seniors 65 and over, $10 for children ages 6 to 17, and free to children under 6 and Fairchild members. Check the Web site for special events throughout the year.

Fairchild Festivals

Fairchild is a goldmine of activity throughout the year. Here are a few events that horticulture lovers should not miss. Admission to most events is $20 for adults, $15 for seniors, and $10 for children 6 to 17. Children five and under as well as members are free. Check the Web site for $5 off admission coupons. If you love plants and homegrown grub, also check out Farmers' Markets (page 104).

Food and Garden Festival

If you're a foodie and love using natural ingredients, head here in March for tips from guests that typically include Food Network names. Food demonstrations, lectures, and plenty 'o local grub can be expected.

International Chocolate Festival

Expect chocolate-y lectures, cooking demonstrations, and tastings every January . . . perhaps not the best way to start a new year.

International Mango Festival

The mango gets a whole new meaning at this weekend festival, typically in mid-July, which pays homage to its Indian heritage. Expect culinary demonstrations, sales of every imaginable mango product, activities, live music, and Bollywood dance performances.

International Orchid Festival

This event typically takes place every May and attracts orchid lovers and sellers from around the country.

Spring Plant Sale

Items from Fairchild's nursery and plant societies throughout the state are on sale during this event, which is typically in late April.

Ichimura Miami-Japan Garden
Watson Island, Miami Beach
www.ci.miami.fl.us

This public park is a genuine Japanese garden recently designed by specialized architects. The pieces within it are Japanese imports that came over in the 1950s when a Japanese man began constructing the space.

The Kampong
4013 Douglas Rd., Coconut Grove
(305) 442-7169
www.ntbg.org/gardens/kampong.php

This seven-acre garden has plant collections that include fruit, palms, and flowering trees, to name a few. Detailed collections are viewable on the Web site. Self-guided tours are open Tues through Thurs from 10 a.m. to 2 p.m. Admission is $15 for adults, $10 for seniors and students with ID, $5 for children ages 4 to 12 and free for children ages three and under.

Miami Beach Botanical Garden
2000 Convention Center Dr., Miami Beach
(305) 673-7256
www.mbgarden.org
Hours: Tues through Sun from 9 a.m. to 5 p.m.

This 4.5-acre garden is usually overlooked by beach-goers. Check the Web site for classes and lectures. There is never an entrance fee.

Pinecrest Gardens
11000 Red Rd., Pinecrest
(305) 669-6942
www.pinecrest-fl.gov

This local space attracts many families with its petting zoo, mini water park, and playground. But there's also a botanic garden on-site as well as a lake.

Vizcaya Museum and Gardens
3251 South Miami Ave., Coconut Grove
(305) 250-9133
www.vizcayamuseum.org

Expert Advice:
Marjie Lambert, Travel Editor,
The Miami Herald

"Fairchild Tropical Botanic Garden has wonderful gardens, but for a cheaper alternative, try **Fruit and Spice Park** in Homestead. I like to see the exotic tropical fruits there, lychees and jackfruit and cashew apples and 150 kinds of mangos. The staff cuts up fruit on the tasting counter, where visitors can sample fruit that is hard to find even at a well-stocked grocery story. Fruit and Spice Park is a one-of-a-kind county park, 37 acres that are divided into geographical regions including Asia, Africa, and Australia. I like to wander around and look at the fruit trees and the herb gardens up close, but visitors can also take a guided tram tour.

"When I need an art fix, I go on gallery walks. My favorites are on the same night in two adjoining areas: The **Design District** and the **Wynwood Arts District,** a few miles north of downtown. Galleries often schedule exhibit openings for the second Sat of the month, when the art walks occur, so visitors have an opportunity to talk to many of the artists whose works are on display. The art is a mix of paintings, drawings, sculpture, art glass, ceramics, and photography, most of it contemporary. About a dozen galleries participate in each of the art walks, so that even in summer, when locals leave town and tourists are scarce, enough galleries are open to fill an evening. Admission is free, and some galleries offer wine and cheese or other nibbles."

Vizcaya was a mansion built by a Miami pioneer, James Deering. He lived on the property from 1916 until his death in 1925. Royalty occupied the halls and you'll feel it; the Mediterranean and European flair reflect in the architecture both indoors and outdoors. The entire property is 180 acres and often plays host to events including weddings and festivals. Take advantage of Free Sundays on the last Sun of the month in July, August, and September. Otherwise, admission is $15 for adults, $10 for students and seniors, and free for children five and under.

PICK **YOUR** OWN

Pick your own is a great inexpensive activity for gardeners and simply lovers of the outdoors alike.

Burr's Berry Farm
12741 SW 216th St., Homestead
(305) 251-0145
www.redlandriot.com

This farm has 30 acres of strawberry plants and is open between Christmas and Mother's Day.

Carpenter's U-Pick Field
Krome Avenue at 292nd Street, Kendall

This is another strawberry joint with no phone or Web site, so take your chances! Giant green peppers are 75 cents each.

Knauss Berry Farm
15980 SW 248th St., Homestead
(305) 247-0668
www.redlandriot.com

The Catch: Cash only.

Strawberries and tomatoes are the specialty here, but don't miss some of the baked goods as well. The cinnamon buns are not to be missed as well as the milkshakes. They are open Mon through Sat from 8:30 a.m. to 5:30 p.m. and from the end of January through early April.

Martha's U-Pic
15755 SW 177th Ave., Kendall

Another strawberry spot, these fields are open from January through May, weather permitting, from 9 a.m. to 5:30 p.m.

GARDENING **RESOURCES**

First, check the Gardening section of *The Miami Herald* (www.miamiherald
.com/living/home), which will provide up-to-date resources on the gardening world in the city.

The Home Depot
www.homedepot.com

Thought this place was just for power tools? Home Depot is actually a great
first stop for cheap gardening supplies. Many locations have a nursery and
ample supplies on-site. Check the Web site for various locations in the city.

MUSEUMS & MEMORIALS:
FREE TO SEE

"That which, perhaps, hears more nonsense than anything in the world, is a picture in a museum."

—*EDMOND DE GONCOURT (1822–1896)*

It's no New York, but Miami holds its own when it comes to museum culture. There's a plethora of free and cheap museums and memorials, which represent the rich diversity in the city. The arts scene alone (also see Art Galleries on page 210) is thriving and there's never a shortage of openings, parties, or cultural events.

ALWAYS FREE

Art Center/South Florida
800/801 Lincoln Rd., Miami Beach
(305) 674-8278
www.artcentersf.org

This is one of the best spots to see art, especially original, in the city. Not only is it free, it serves as the home to new artists so you'll get to see lots of upcoming talent before they are public and receptions are often held in the space. Check the Web site for schedules, artists currently in residence, and events. Hours vary.

Bacardi Museum
2100 Biscayne Blvd., North Miami
(305) 573-8600

The Catch: You must make an appointment pre-visit.

This seems like an appropriate place to go on a beach vacation, in addition to the fact that it's free year-round. Tours are available by appointment.

Bakehouse Art Complex
561 NW 32nd St., Downtown Miami
(305) 576-2828
www.bacfl.org

This non-profit organization hosts upcoming and "mid-career" artists and gives them an affordable workplace and exhibition space. Current artists are searchable on the Web site by name or medium and you'll have no problem finding something you like; architecture, ceramics, painting, photography, and sculpture are only a few types of art represented. Entrance is always free. Open daily from noon to 5 p.m.

Black Police Precinct and Court House Museum
480 NW 11 St., Downtown Miami
(305) 329-2513
www.miamigov.com

This probably won't top your vacation list, but a visit will yield some unique history lessons. This museum, opened in 2009, details the history of the building itself and the retired officers who influenced integration in Miami. Open Tues through Fri from 10 a.m. to 5 p.m.

Cuba at the Bay of Pigs Museum
1821 SW 9th St., Little Havana
(305) 649-4719

Admission is always free at this historical museum, which chronicles the history of the Bay of Pigs and the exile community in Miami. Open Mon through Fri from 9 a.m. to 4 p.m.

Gold Coast Railroad Museum
12450 SW 152nd St., Kendall
(305) 253-0063
http://gcrm.org

Train-o-philes could spend an entire day at this museum, which is dedicated the history of South Florida's railroads and train travel in general. Do not miss participating in model train building, which takes place on weekends from 11 a.m. to 4 p.m. and weekdays (excluding Mon) from 11 a.m. to 2 p.m. In addition to free admission on the first Sat of every month, the museum offers free rides on their Edwin Link 2-foot gauge train on Wed at 11 a.m. and 1 p.m. The first Sat of every month is free; admission is otherwise $6 for adults, $4 for children ages 3 to 12, and free for children under 3. Open Sat and Sun from 11 a.m. to 4 p.m.; Tues, Wed, and Fri from 10 a.m. to 4 p.m.; Thurs from 10 a.m. to 7 p.m.; closed Mon.

The Holocaust Memorial

1933–1945 Meridian Ave., Miami Beach
(305) 538-1663
www.holocaustmmb.org

This memorable memorial is always free but is bound to leave you with ever-lasting impressions. The iconic hand centerpiece can be seen from afar and elicits emotional responses from viewers. Walk through the space and learn about the Holocaust and its victims. Open daily from 9 a.m. to 5 p.m.

The Patricia and Phillip Frost Art Museum

10975 SW 17 St., Sweetwater area
(305) 348-2890
http://thefrost.fiu.edu

The Catch: Parking is tricky on this campus so don't mistake a seemingly open spot for a free one; it's probably reserved for students and will result in a ticket. Instead, park in the metered stalls around campus.

This free museum at Florida International University's University Park campus is a Smithsonian affiliate that exhibits a variety of paintings, sculptures, and other types of art. It is always free and open to the public. Open Tues through Sat from 10 a.m. to 5 p.m.; Sun from noon to 5 p.m.; closed Mon and certain school breaks and holidays.

SOMETIMES **FREE** (OR **JUST** CHEAP)

The Bass Museum

2121 Park Ave., Miami Beach
(305) 673-7530
www.bassmuseum.org

This museum has some serious stuff. One recent addition was the Egyptian mummy gallery, which opened in April 2010. Concerts and talks are held year-round and are updated on the online schedule. During Miami Museum Month, Bass participated in a buy one, get one free deal. Typically admission is $8 for adults, $6 for seniors and students with ID, and free for members

Florida History

If you're a history buff, swing by any of these city-sponsored exhibits, most of which are free and open to the public during regular business hours.

City of Coral Gables City Hall

405 Biltmore Way, Coral Gables

(305) 446-6800

www.coralgables.com

Check out the historical display, which is free and chronicles the city's history.

City of North Miami Beach City Hall

17011 NE 19th Ave., North Miami Beach

(305) 947-7581

www.citynmb.com

Similar to the Coral Gables display, check out the history of this part of northern Miami.

Historical Museum

101 West Flagler St., Miami

(305) 375-1492

This museum has at least one free day a week; call for information.

Miami Dade Public Library Florida Collection

101 West Flagler St., Miami

This library has a terrific south Florida collection on its second floor.

Sunny Isles Beach City Hall

18070 Collins Ave., Sunny Isles Beach

Sunny Isles' City Hall has a beautiful and large Hall of History, with no charge to view!

and children under six. Check out the snack bar for munchies and free Wi-Fi. Open Wed through Sun from noon to 5 p.m.; closed Mon and Tues.

Haitian Heritage Museum
4141 NE 2nd Ave., Suite 105C, Downtown Miami
(305) 371-5988
www.haitianheritagemuseum.org

This non-profit duly dedicates itself to paying homage to Haiti's rich culture. Admission is $7 for adults and $5 for students with ID. Consider a membership if you'll revisit; the $15 student membership includes admission to one Museum Series Event, one Art Exhibit event, and advance notice of the museum's seminar series. Open Tues through Fri from 10 a.m. to 5 p.m.; closed Sat through Mon.

Historical Museum of Southern Florida
101 West Flagler St., Miami
(305) 375-1492
www.hmsf.org

If possible, check out this museum on the second Sat of every month or the third Thurs after 5 p.m., as it's free for the public. Sun is Contribution Day. Otherwise, admission is $8 for adults, $7 for seniors and students with ID, $5 for children from 6 to 12 years old, and free for members and children under 6. Buy a $10 ticket for the Miami Art Museum and visit both in one shot. Open Tues through Fri from 10 a.m. to 5 p.m.; third Thurs until 9 p.m.; Sat and Sun from noon to 5 p.m.; closed Mon.

Jewish Museum of Florida
301 Washington Ave., Miami Beach
(305) 672-5044
www.jewishmuseum.com

Take advantage of free Sat before you visit another day; otherwise admission is $6 for adults, $5 for seniors, and free for children under six years old. Print a $1 discount coupon on the Web site. Open Tues through Sun from 10 a.m. to 5 p.m.; closed on Mon and civil and Jewish holidays.

Lowe Art Museum

1301 Stanford Dr., Coral Gables
(305) 284-3603
www6.miami.edu/lowe

Part of the University of Miami, the collection includes pieces from Asia, Africa, Europe, and the Americas and is always free for university-affiliated people with ID and children under 12. Admission is otherwise $10 for adults, $5 for students, seniors, or groups with more than 10 people. Educational groups from kindergarten through college with groups over 10 get in for $3 each. Check the Web site for scheduled lectures and events throughout the year. Open Tues through Sat from 10 a.m. to 4 p.m.; Sun from noon to 4 p.m.; closed on Mon and university holidays.

Merrick House

907 Coral Way, Coral Gables
(305) 460-5361
www.coralgables.com

This house, the childhood home of George Merrick, pays homage to the man who founded the City of Coral Gables. Built at the end of the 19th century, the house maintains a 1920s appearance preserving the history of Merrick's life as a site on the National Register of Historic Places. Admission is $5 for adults; $3 for seniors, students, and tour groups; $1 for children 6 to 12; and free for children 5 and under. Tours, which are approximately 45 minutes, occur Wed at 1, 2 and 3 p.m. and Sun at the same times.

Miami Museum Month

Miami Museum Month (www.miamimuseummonth.com), which is typically held in May, is the best time to explore the city's offerings and take advantage of specials that participating museums offer. Offers typically include buy one, get one free admission and special events. Check the Web site for participating museums, which vary yearly.

Miami Art Museum
101 West Flagler St., Miami
(305) 375-3000
www.miamiartmuseum.org

Every Sun and every second Sat of the month the museum is free, and is always that way for kids and students. Otherwise, adult admission is $8. Also keep an eye on their Web site for free and cheap events and lectures. Open Tues through Fri from 10 a.m. to 5 p.m.; Sat and Sun from noon to 5 p.m.

Miami Science Museum
3280 South Miami Ave., Coconut Grove
(305) 646-4200
www.miamisci.org

This is the local favorite science museum, which has rotating exhibits throughout the year and frequent events, including star shows in their planetarium on the first Fri of every month. Admission prices vary by residency status. Adult admission is $14.95 or $12.70 for residents; $10.95 for seniors, students with ID, and children ages 3 to 12 and $9.30 for residents. Children under three and members are always free. Open daily from 10 a.m. to 6 p.m.

Museum of Contemporary Art
770 NE 125th St., North Miami
(305) 893-6211
www.mocanomi.org

Visit the last Fri of each month from 7 p.m. to 10 p.m. for Jazz at MoCA. Admission is $5 for adults, $3 for students and seniors, and free all the time for MoCA members, children under 12, and North Miami residents and city employees. Open Tues, Thurs, Fri, and Sat from 11 a.m. to 5 p.m.; Wed from 1 to 9 p.m.; Sun from noon to 5 p.m.; closed Mon.

Vizcaya Museum and Gardens
3251 South Miami Ave., Coconut Grove
(305) 250-9133
www.vizcayamuseum.org

This national historic landmark is the former estate of Miami industrialist James Deering. Think mini Versailles—a grand main house and 10 acres of gardens. Aside from Free Sundays, when the museum opens its doors the last Sun of the month for July, August, and September, admission is $15 per adult year-round. Aside from this place being so worth the $15, students, seniors, and residents get discounted admission for $10 or under and children five and under always get in free. Open daily from 9:30 a.m. to 4:30 p.m.

The Wolfsonian Museum
1001 Washington Ave., Miami Beach
(305) 531-1001
www.wolfsonian.org

Florida International University's museum features a collection that highlights the modern era from 1885 to 1945 and "focuses on how art and design shape and reflect the human experience." If possible, go Fri after 6 p.m. when admission is free. Otherwise, admission is $7 for adults; $5 for seniors, students with valid ID, and children; and free for children under six as well as students, faculty, and staff of the university. Hours vary by season. Summer hours are Thurs from noon to 6 p.m.; Fri from noon to 9 p.m.; Sat and Sun from noon to 6 p.m.; closed Mon through Wed.

World Erotic Art Museum
1205 Washington Ave., Miami Beach
(305) 532-9336
www.weam.com

No surprises or elusive name here! The space has more than 20 rooms and is more than 20,000 square feet, so you're bound to be entertained. Open Mon through Thurs from 11 a.m. to 10 p.m.; Fri through Sun from 11 a.m. to 12 midnight.

TOURS:
THE (FREE)DOM TRAIL

"I was recently on a tour of Latin America, and the only regret I have was that I didn't study Latin harder in school so I could converse with those people."

—DAN QUAYLE

Whether you're a tourist or a local, taking tours always seems like forfeiting our ability to blend in. But sometimes it is seriously worth it—especially if it's free. Miami is a goldmine of history, so whether you're a tourist or local, just accept the fact that you'll likely never know all of it. So take advantage of the free and/or cheap tours around the city throughout the year. And if you are really resistant, try a self-guided tour. And ditch the fanny pack.

FREE, **CHEAP,** & SELF-GUIDED **TOURS**

The Barnacle Historic State Park
3485 Main Hwy., Coconut Grove
(305) 442-6866
www.floridastateparks.org

Guided tours are $3 for adults, $1 for children 6 to 12, and free for children 5 and under. Fri through Mon tours are at 10 and 11:30 a.m. and 1 and 2:30 p.m. Wed and Thurs tours are available but require advance reservations.

Bill Baggs Cape Florida State Park
1200 South Crandon Blvd., Key Biscayne
(305) 361-5811
www.floridastateparks.org/capeflorida

The Catch: There's a parking fee that's $4 for a single occupant and $8 for two or more occupants

On Tues through Mon, tours led by park rangers are offered at 10 a.m. and 1 p.m. The park itself is open from 8 a.m. to around 7 p.m. (or whenever sunset happens to be) daily and throughout the year.

Biltmore Hotel
1200 Anastasia Ave., Coral Gables
(305) 445-1926
www.biltmorehotel.com

Free tours are given at this historic hotel on Sun afternoons at 1:30, 2:20 and 3:30 p.m. Listen to professional storytellers recount the days when the

Biltmore was a celebrity hotspot and attracted names like Ginger Rogers and Al Capone.

Crandon Park
4000 Crandon Park Blvd., Key Biscayne

An admission fee of $5 gets you into the park in addition to a tour of the area. There is a two-mile beach, swimming, picnic, and concession area. The Crandon Park Beach Amusement Center has a carousel, outdoor skating rink, splash fountain, and a playground; the Crandon Park Beach Gardens features lakes and ample outdoor space.

Little Havana
Calle Ocho (8th Street), Little Havana

On the last Fri of every from 6:30 to 11 p.m., the streets light up for Viernes Culturales, an outdoor festival that integrates the arts and culture of this historic Miami neighborhood. Take advantage of free walking tours of the neighborhood.

Miami Design Preservation League

The MDPL has a slew of awesome tour options.

Local historians, architects, and natives lead 90-minute guided tours throughout the beach. They typically depart from the Art Deco Gift Shop at 10th Street and Ocean Drive in the Ocean Auditorium's Art Deco Welcome Center daily at 10:30 a.m. and Thurs at 6:30 p.m. only.

Self-guided tours are also an option, from 9:30 a.m. to 5 p.m. starting at the Gift Shop. The shop lends you an iPod (which must be returned by 7 p.m.) as well as a map, which will guide you around the area and typically takes between one and two hours. Another option: for $10, use your own cell phone for a self-guided tour by calling (786) 312-1229.

Contact the MDPL for more information at (305) 672-2014 or www.mdpl.org.

Simpson Park
www.miamigov.com

Near Downtown Miami, this forest area has been restored as a public space for visitors wishing to picnic and ponder outdoors.

Virginia Key Beach Park
4020 Virginia Beach Dr., Key Biscayne
(305) 960-4600
www.virginiakeybeachpark.net

Download the guidebook on the Web site for a self-guided tour around the premises, which is home to a variety of plant and endangered animal species.

Vizcaya Museum and Gardens
3251 South Miami Ave., Coconut Grove
(305) 250-9133
www.vizcayamuseum.org

On the last Sun in July, August, and September, this Miami landmark holds Free Sundays, which invite the community in for free tours, lectures and arts.

GETTING **WILD** ON **THE** CHEAP

Everglades National Park
40001 State Rd. 9336 at the Ernest Coe Visitor Center, Homestead
(305) 242-7700
www.nps.gov/ever

Skip the man-made (and expensive) establishments and check out the most real zoo there is: the Everglades. You should also visit because this park is fast disappearing as a result of land development, but many efforts have been made to preserve the natural wildlife and habitats that exist. Charges are minimal: $10 for a private vehicle, $5 for pedestrians and cyclists, and

---

South Beach for a Quarter

If you're spending the day on South Beach, utilize the ultimate cheap bastard's tool: 25 cent transportation. There's a goldmine of sites to see everywhere around the southern part of Miami Beach, especially, which boasts original deco architecture and various historic sites.

The air-conditioned shuttle runs every 20 minutes from 7:40 a.m. to 10 a.m. Mon through Sat, every 12 minutes from 10 a.m. to 6 p.m., and every 20 minutes from 6 p.m. to 1 a.m. On Sun and holidays the schedule is 10 a.m. to noon every 20 minutes, every 12 minutes from noon to 6 p.m., and every 20 minutes from 6 p.m. to 1 a.m. It makes stops around the entire beach area along south Alton Road until 6th Street, West Avenue, Washington Avenue, and a few other stops as far north as 17th Street and Dade Boulevard. Call (305) 770-3131 for more information.

$25 for an annual pass from the date of purchase. Hiking, fishing, boating, and canoeing are a few options for visitors. Start at the Visitor Center, which is open from 9 a.m. to 5 p.m. daily, to ask about more activities and information.

Marjory Stoneman Douglas Biscayne Nature Center
6767 Crandon Blvd. at Crandon Park, Key Biscayne
(305) 361-6767
www.biscaynenaturecenter.org

Various activities at this community center are only $10 per person including Sea Grass Adventures, which pairs guests with a naturalist to identify the species in catch-and-release nets. There's also the Hammock Hike, Beach Babies, Coastal Ecology, and Fossil Reef Tide Pool.

Pinecrest Gardens
11000 Red Rd., Pinecrest
(305) 669-6942
www.pinecrest-fl.gov

Parrot Jungle formerly occupied this space, which is now free daily from 8 a.m. to sunset. For $3 children ages 2 to 12 can enjoy the Splash 'N' Play mini water park from 10 a.m. until an hour before closing. There's also a traditional playground and petting zoo open daily at 10 a.m., noon , 2 p.m., and 4 p.m. Adults and children alike utilize the botanical gardens and lake.

PEOPLE-**WATCHING** PARADISE

If you don't want to shell out the 10 bucks or deal with unfortunate drink minimums at comedy clubs, you will not be deprived of humor anywhere in Miami Beach, especially. Here are a few of the city's best spots for self-guided tours and people-watching, which are guaranteed to yield some form of entertainment.

Collins Avenue
Between South Pointe Park and North Miami Beach

A Collins Avenue drive will yield a vast array of Miami Beach life. Also known as State Road A1A, Collins runs from South Beach's southernmost point through to North Miami Beach. Optimal people-watching is from the park through about 20th Street, where a slew of Miami's most coveted and historical art deco hotels are; the Shore Club, Shelbourne, the Raleigh, and Delano are among them. During the day, peek inside the hotel lobbies and take advantage of poolside space (if it's open) where celebrity sightings aren't unusual. Likewise, debauchery ensues at most of these hotels nightly; just be prepared that some flashy nightlife attire in Miami doesn't cover much more than bathing suits.

Española Way
Between Jefferson Avenue and Collins Avenue

Miami natives know about Española Way, a true, tucked-away Miami gem. Some of the Mediterranean-style buildings in the historic Spanish village date back to the 1920s. Music almost always fills the space, which is already filled with outdoor drinking and funky boutiques. Every weekend is an open-air market, the Española Way Weekend Festival, where you'll inevitably see some of Miami Beach's best characters.

Lincoln Road
Between Collins Avenue and Alton Road

There's no shortage of all forms of eye candy on Lincoln Road, where outdoor seating dominates the landscape. A hodgepodge of people congregate here: teenagers confined to the movie theater area, families strolling around, Miami's finest shopping for the mini-dress of the night, as well as street performers (with or without street festivals going on). Van Dyke and Nexxt Café are two well-known Miami eateries (and drinkeries) that will typically allow you to snag outdoor seats with only the purchase of a drink, during the day especially.

Ocean Drive
Between South Pointe Drive and 15th Street

You may remember the 2006 MTV reality show *8th and Ocean,* which chronicled the inner workings of a high-fashion Miami modeling agency that is still in the same spot. Just beyond that is the famous News Café. Ocean Drive is a see-and-be-seen street, which makes it a short stretch where an afternoon can easily be spent. Starting at South Pointe Drive heading north, you'll pass Nikki Beach, a Miami (and international) party spot that almost always attracts see-and-be-seen-ers. Zigzag onto the beach and stroll north. Past 11th and Ocean is the Versace Mansion and several famous art deco–style hotels that are always fun to look at, in addition to their diverse clientele. At 15th Street, you can cut over to the beach (where it goes without saying that there's plenty to admire) and then over to Lincoln Road, which is after 16th Street.

TRANSPORTATION:
ON THE ROAD AGAIN

"Travel is only glamorous in retrospect."

—*PAUL THEROUX*

Until writing this chapter, I was under the impression that homeless people were the only ones who used Miami's public transportation. With the exception of the Metrorail and the TriRail, the only semi-smart transportation inventions in the city, I never stepped foot on a bus during the 20-plus years I resided in Miami. Unless you intend to stay on the beach or have monk-like patience, a car is the easiest way to go.

Locals must get around by car, so South Beach visitors who want to venture to other areas may want to consider car rentals equipped with a solid GPS. Miami isn't an easy city to navigate if you aren't familiar with the layout. If you do rent a car, first check into the parking situation; there are a few hotels that offer free parking. If it's not free, plan to pay an arm and a leg for parking or try to arrange a day-long rental.

BUS, **TRAIN,** PUBLIC **TRANSIT** . . . OH MY!

Most of the below modes of transportation are managed by the City of Miami Dade (www.miamidade.gov); customer service can be reached at (305) 891-3131.

Metrobus

Bus lines run throughout the entire city. Check the Miami Dade Web site (www.miamidade.gov) for routes and time schedules. The fare of $2 per trip is cheaper than New York City!

Metromover

I'd never heard of this in my life, but it's FREE! The route starts around Brickell and runs up to the Adrienne Arsht Performing Arts Center, which could potentially save you some parking money.

Metrorail

The above-ground subway runs from Dadeland, which is in the Kendall/South Miami area, up to Hialeah, which is a bit north of Miami proper. Sadly,

The Buses You Do Want to Take

Brickell Key Shuttle
www.brickellarea.com/maps_transit.html
Hours: Mon through Sat from 6:30 a.m. to 6:30 p.m. every 15 minutes
Take advantage of the air-conditioned 25 cent shuttle that operates between the local Metrorail/Metromover station and Brickell Key. Stops are made along Coral Way, SW 2nd Avenue, SW 8th and 10th streets, Brickell Avenue, and Brickell Bay Drive.

South Beach Local
(305) 770-3131
www.miamibeach.gov
Hours: Every 20 minutes from 7:40 a.m. to 10 a.m. Mon through Sat, every 12 minutes from 10 a.m. to 6 p.m., and every 20 minutes from 6 p.m. to 1 a.m.; on Sun and holidays, 10 a.m. to noon every 20 minutes, every 12 minutes from noon to 6 p.m., and every 20 minutes from 6 p.m. to 1 a.m.
South Beach also has a 25 cent shuttle that runs south Alton Road until 6th Street, West Avenue, Washington Avenue, and a few other stops as far north as 17th Street and Dade Boulevard.

this can't be taken to any airport and you'll have to walk a bit to get to the station. Fares are $2 per ride.

Tri-Rail
(800) TRI-RAIL (874-7245)
www.tri-rail.com

Fares are based on travel distance, all of which are affordable and worthwhile. You can take this from Miami International Airport all the way up to West Palm Beach. Ft Lauderdale Airport is almost halfway between, so it's a great money (and time!) saver if you're making the trek.

TO & FROM **AIRPORTS** & **AMTRAK**

If you're staying at a hotel, your first pre-trip call should be checking to see if there is free transportation for hotel guests. Many hotels do offer this service, and it should be completely exploited if possible. Other options to get to and from the airport are below.

Airport Flyer
(305) 468-5900
www.miamidade.gov

Expert Advice:
Peter Greenberg,
Travel Editor of CBS News

"Whenever possible, I avoid flying out of or through MIA. It's like the last flight out of Saigon over there. Instead, opt for Miami's "alternate airport," **Fort Lauderdale-Hollywood International.** You just find better fares and a lot better experience. When I am in Miami International Airport, though, I make a point to stop at **La Carreta,** which serves authentic Cuban food at very reasonable prices. Even better, stop by the original location in Little Havana to really experience the local scene.

"**Books & Books** is one of the top independent bookstores in the area with a few locations to choose from. It's great for browsing through the interesting collection of art books or to sit in on a book talk (they draw well-known authors as well as local favorites).

"Here's a little-known tip: the **South Beach Local bus** offers **25 cent transportation** around the South Beach. It's much easier than dealing pricey taxi cabs and it zips around the beach every 10 to 15 minutes until 1 a.m. **Monty's Marina Coconut Grove** is known more for its marina location than its food, but what a view! The raw bar is probably your best bet, and if you want to avoid the maddening crowds, don't go on a weekend night."

A new express bus provided by the city starts at $2.35 each way to and from Miami Beach. There's also a connection at a Metrorail so those going downtown can connect easily. The Flyer runs every 30 minutes daily from 6 a.m. to 11 p.m. and has luggage racks available.

Airport Super Express
(305) 807-0270
http://airportsuperexpress.com

The Catch: Reservations must be made 24 hours in advance. Don't assume you're confirmed only if you've sent the request. You must get a confirmation.

This is mostly a good deal if you're traveling in groups, as rates are based on numbers of people rather than individuals. One-way trips to and from Miami International Airport and Miami Beach start at $45 for one to four people ($11.25 each before tip if you're riding with four people.) Call or e-mail reservations@airportsuperexpress.com for reservations.

Super Shuttle
(305) 871-2000
www.supershuttle.com

The Catch: Because multiple pickups are made in vans, the company usually makes your pickup time way earlier than necessary for to-airport rides based on your departure time. If you feel the time is unreasonably early, adjust your departure time—at your own risk, of course.

I can personally attest to this company as I've used them in multiple cities; Miami being one of them. They are always on time, if not early, and rates, which are based on distance, are always reasonable.

Get Outta Town

There's plenty to do in Miami, but if you've already hit it all, check out flight specials on airlines like Jet Blue and Spirit. Once in a while, an unbelievable fare sale will happen. For example: $15 to Puerto Rico or under $100 each way to Central America. Your best bet is to check Kayak.com.

Tri-Rail
www.tri-rail.com

This rail line starts at Miami International Airport and goes north through Palm Beach County. This is a great option for those flying out of airports north of Miami, which are sometimes cheaper based on destination. The one-way fare from Miami International Airport to Fort Lauderdale Airport is only $3.75, which is cheaper than gas and less time than catching a ride. Fares are based on distance so expect it to be a bit higher if you're going further from your destination.

APPENDIX A:

FESTIVALS & ANNUAL EVENTS

FILM

American Black Film Festival; (646) 375-2059; www.abff.com
Doc Miami International Film Festival; http://docmiami.org
Fort Lauderdale International Film Festival; (954) 760-9898; www.fliff
.com
Gay and Lesbian Film Festival; (305) 534-9924; www.mglff.com
The Israel Film Festival; www.mi.israelfilmfestival.com
Italian Film Festival; www.cinemaitaly.com
Miami International Film Festival; (305) 237-3456; www.miamifilm
festival.com
Miami Jewish Film Festival; (305) 573-7305; www.miamijewishfilmfestival
.com
Miami Short Film Festival; (305) 586-8105; www.miamishortfilmfestival
.com
Romance In a Can; www.romanceinacan.com
Women's International Film Festival; (305) 653-9700; www.womensfilm
fest.com

MUSIC

Festival Miami; (305) 284-4940; www.music.miami.edu
Greynolds Park Love-In; (305) 945-3425; www.miamidade.gov/greynolds
lovein
Heineken Transatlantic Festival; www.rhythmfoundation.com
Mainly Mozart Festival; www.mainlymozart.com
Miami International Piano Festival; www.miamipianofest.com

The Miami Music Festival; www.miamimusicfestival.org
Sunfest Music Festival; (800) SUNFEST (786-3378); www.sunfest.com
Ultra Music Festival; www.ultramusicfestival.com

MISCELLANEOUS

ARTS

Art Basel; (305) 674-1292; www.artbaselmiamibeach.com
Art Deco Weekend Festival; www.mdpl.org
Art in the Park; (305) 644-8888; www.carnavalmiami.com/artinthe
parkconcerts
Aqua Girl; www.aquagirl.org
Beaux Arts Annual Festival of Arts; www.beauxartsmiami.org
Caribbean Festival; (305) 665-5379; www.bobmarleymovement.com
Coconut Grove Arts Festival; (305) 447-0401; www.coconutgrovearts
fest.com
Columbus Day Regatta; www.columbusdayregatta.net
Dade Heritage Days; www.dadeheritagetrust.org
Family Fun Fest; (305) 230-PARK (7275)
Gay Pride; www.miamibeachgaypride.com
Goombay Festival; www.goombayfestivalcoconutgrove.com
International Ballet Festival; (305) 549-7711; www.internationalballet
festival.com
Mercedes-Benz Fashion Week; www.mbfashionweek.com
Miami Attractions Month; www.amazingmiamiattractions.com
Miami Beach Antique Jewelry and Watch Show; www.miamibeachantique
jewelryandwatchshow.com
Miami Beach Antique Show; (239) 732-6642; www.originalmiamibeach
antiqueshow.com
Miami Book Fair International; www.miamibookfair.com
Miami Carnival; miamicarnival.net
Miami International Agriculture and Cattle Show; (305) 228-3414; www
.miacs.info

Miami International Boat Show and Strictly Sail; www.miamiboatshow
.com

Miami Museum Month; www.miamimuseummonth.com

Miami Riverday Commission; (305) 644-0544; www.miamirivercommission
.org

Miami Spa Month; www.miamispamonth.com

Orange Bowl Fan Fest; www.orangebowl.org

Redland International Orchid Show; www.redlandorchidfestival.org

Sleepless Night; (305) 673-7577; www.sleeplessnight.org

South Beach Comedy Festival; www.soutbeachcomedyfestival.com

South Miami Rotary Art Festival; www.southmiamiartfest.org

The Summer Groove; www.thesummergroove.com

Swap Miami; www.swapmiami.com

Viernes Culturales (Cultural Fridays); (305) 643-5500; www.viernes
culturales.org

VolleyPalooza; www.southbeachvolleyball.com

White Party Week; www.whiteparty.org

FOOD

Harvest Festival; (386) 860-0092; www.miamiharvest.webs.com

International Chocolate Festival; (305) 667-1651; www.fairchildgarden.org

Miami Food and Wine Festival; (305) 371-WINE; www.miamiwinefestival
.org

Miami Goin' Green Earth Day Festival; www.miamigoingreen.com

Miami Spice; www.ilovemiamispice.com

Miami Street Food Festival; http://miamistreetfoodfest.com

Oktoberfest; (305) 774-1883; www.bierhaus.cc

Redland Summer Fruit Festival; www.fruitandspicepark.org

Rib and Beer Fest; (305) 774-1883; www.bierhaus.cc

Saint Sophia Greek Festival; (305) 854-2922; www.saintsophiagreek
festival.com

South Beach Food and Wine Festival; www.sobewineandfoodfest.com

APPENDIX B:

NEIGHBORHOOD RESOURCES

Miami Dade County (www.miamidade.gov) is the head honcho when it comes to the county as a whole, but the below local governments constitute specific neighborhoods throughout the city. Their official Web sites will give further details about local happenings and events.

Aventura, www.cityofaventura.com
Bal Harbour, www.balharbourgov.com
Bay Harbor Islands, www.bayharborislands.org
Biscayne Park, www.biscayneparkfl.gov
Coral Gables, www.coralgables.com
Cutler Bay, www.cutlerbay-fl.gov
Doral, www.cityofdoral-fl.gov
El Portal, http://elportalvillage.com
Florida City, www.floridacityfl.us
Golden Beach, www.goldenbeach.us
Hialeah, www.hialeahfl.gov
Hialeah Gardens, www.cityofhialeahgardens.org
Homestead, www.cityofhomestead.com
Indian Creek, www.icvps.org
Key Biscayne, www.keybiscayne.fl.gov
Medley Miami, www.townofmedley.com
Miami Beach, www.miamibeachfl.gov
Miami Gardens, www.miamigardens-fl.gov
Miami Lakes, miamilakes-fl.gov
Miami Shores, www.miamishoresvillage.com
Miami Springs, www.miamisprings-fl.gov
North Bay Village, www.nbvillage.com
North Miami, www.northmiamifl.gov
North Miami Beach, www.citynmb.com
Opa-locka, www.opalockafl.gov
Palmetto Bay, www.palmettobay-fl.gov

Pinecrest, www.pinecrest-fl.gov
South Miami, www.cityofsouthmiami.net
Sunny Isles Beach, www.sibfl.net
Surfside, www.townofsurfsidefl.gov
Sweetwater, www.cityofsweetwater.fl.gov
Virginia Gardens, www.virginiagardens-fl.gov

APPENDIX C:

LOCAL MEDIA

Yes, newspapers do still exist in print. And I'm all for them in Miami, especially, because many publications are free. Grab a copy of local papers or check out Web sites for schedules of events, festivals, and community happenings. Many are free and available in local stores or stands; others can be purchased cheaply or viewed for free online.

Daily Business Review
www.dailybusinessreview.com

While it might not be the most useful resource for free and cheap activities, it is free itself online, which is a perk.

Miami Community Newspapers
www.communitynewspapers.com

Twelve local papers are part of this conglomerate, which distributes them for free around each city. These include: Aventura, Coconut Grove, Coral Gables, Cutler Bay, Doral, Homestead, Kendall, Miami Gardens, Palmetto Bay, Pinecrest, South Miami, and Sunny Isles. Check the Web site to view any issue, which lists community events and happenings.

The Miami Herald
www.miamiherald.com

The *Miami Herald* costs 50 cents per day and is free online. *El Nuevo Herald* is the Spanish language version of the paper, which is also available daily. Both papers are published daily and updated online frequently.

Miami New Times
www.miaminewtimes.com

This paper is the city's alternative weekly, which lists a variety of local events and news. It's distributed on Thurs and is available for free throughout the city; weed through the sex ads in the back to read sex column Savage Love.

Miami Today News
www.miamitodaynews.com

The paper is free online and has a handy calendar that's listed by topics.

Natural Awakenings
www.namiami.com

You'll see it for free around the city, so grab a copy if you're a health nut especially. The publication lists local events and articles with a natural twist.

South Beach News
www.southbeachnews.tv

Read the online newspaper and watch on-location broadcasts discussing local news and events. A calendar is listed on the site.

South Florida Sun-Sentinel
www.sun-sentinel.com

It's the northern version of *the Miami Herald*, which covers Fort Lauderdale and areas further north.

APPENDIX D

PUBLIC LIBRARIES

Main Library
101 West Flagler St., Miami
(305) 375-2665

Allapattah Branch
1799 NW 35th St., NW Miami
(305) 638-6086

California Club Branch
850 Ives Dairy Rd., NE Miami
(305) 770-3155

Civic Center Branch
1501 NW 12th Ave., NW Miami
(305) 324-0291

Coconut Grove Branch
2875 McFarlane Rd., Coconut Grove
(305) 442-8695

Concord Branch
3882 SW 112th Ave., West Miami
(305) 207-1344

Coral Gables Branch
3443 Segovia St., Coral Gables
(305) 442-8706

Coral Reef Branch
9211 Coral Reef Dr., Kendall
(305) 233-8324

Country Walk Branch
15433 SW 137th Ave., Kendall
(786) 293-4577

Culmer/Overtown Branch
350 NW 13th St., Overtown
(305) 579-5322

Doral Branch
10785 NW 58th St., Doral
(305) 716-9598

Edison Center Branch
531 NW 62nd St., Little Haiti
(305) 757-0668

Fairlawn Branch
6376 SW 8th St., West Miami
(305) 261-1571

Golden Glades Branch
100 NE 166th St., NE Miami
(305) 787-1544

Hispanic Branch
2190 West Flagler St., Little Havana
(305) 541-9444

Homestead Branch
700 North Homestead Blvd.,
Homestead
(305) 246-0168

International Mall Branch
10315 NW 12th St., Doral
(305) 594-2514

Kendale Lakes Branch
15205 SW 88th St., West Kendall
(305) 388-0326

Kendall Branch
9101 SW 97th Ave., Kendall
(305) 279-0520

Key Biscayne Branch
299 Crandon Blvd., Key Biscayne
(305) 361-6134

Lakes of the Meadow Branch
4284 SW 152nd Ave., West Kendall
(305) 222-2149

Lemon City Branch
430 NE 61st St., NE Miami
(305) 757-0662

Little River Branch
160 NE 79th St., NE Miami
(305) 751-8689

Miami Beach Regional
227 22nd St., Miami Beach
(305) 535-4219

Miami Lakes Branch
6699 Windmill Gate Rd., Miami
Lakes
(305) 822-6520

Miami Springs Branch
700 South Royal Poinciana Blvd.,
Suite 103, Miami Springs
(305) 884-2575

Model City Branch
2211 NW 54th St., NW Miami
(305) 636-2233

North Central Branch
9590 NW 27th Ave., NW Miami
(305) 693-4541

North Dade Regional
2455 NW 183rd St., Miami Gardens
(305) 625-6424

North Shore Branch
7501 Collins Ave., Miami Beach
(305) 864-5392

Northeast Branch
19200 West Country Club Dr.,
Aventura
(305) 931-5512

Opa-locka Branch
780 Fisherman St., Suite 140,
Opa-locka
(305) 688-1134

Palm Springs North Branch
17601 NW 78th Ave., Hialeah
(305) 820-8564

Palmetto Bay Branch
17641 Old Cutler Rd., Palmetto Bay
(305) 232-1771

Pinecrest Branch
5835 SW 111th St., Pinecrest
(305) 668-4571

Shenandoah Branch
2111 SW 19th St., Miami
(305) 898-6994

South Dade Regional
10750 SW 211th St., SW Miami
(305) 233-8140

South Miami Branch
6000 Sunset Dr., South Miami
(305) 667-6121

South Shore Branch
131 Alton Rd., Miami Beach
(305) 535-4223

Sunny Isles Beach Branch
18070 Collins Ave., Sunny Isles
Beach
(305) 682-0726

Sunset Branch
10855 SW 72nd St., Suite 13,
South Miami
(305) 270-6368

Tamiami Branch
13250 SW 8th St., West Miami
(305) 223-4758

Virrick Park Branch
3255 Plaza St., Coconut Grove
(305) 442-7872

West Dade Regional
9445 Coral Way, West Miami
(305) 553-1134

West Flagler Branch
5050 West Flagler St., West Miami
(305) 442-8710

West Kendall Regional
10201 Hammocks Blvd., Kendall
(305) 385-7135

INDEX

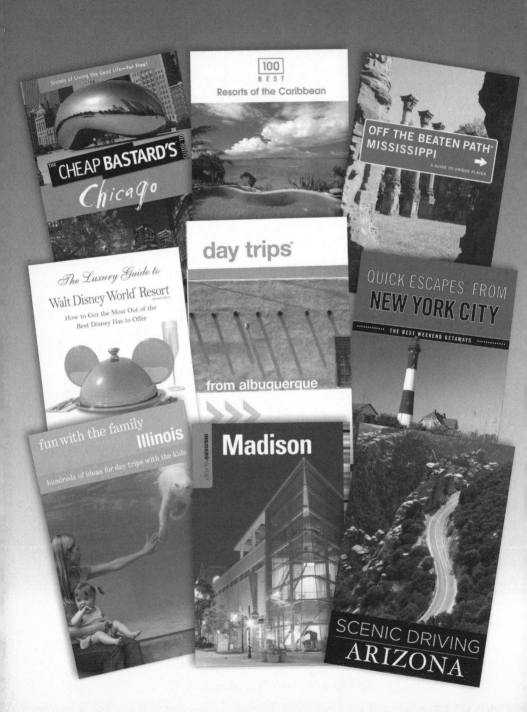

INSIDERS' GUIDE®

The acclaimed travel series that has sold more than 2 million copies!

Discover: Your Travel Destination. Your Home. Your Home-to-Be.

Albuquerque

Anchorage & Southcentral Alaska

Atlanta

Austin

Baltimore

Baton Rouge

Boulder & Rocky Mountain National Park

Branson & the Ozark Mountains

California's Wine Country

Cape Cod & the Islands

Charleston

Charlotte

Chicago

Cincinnati

Civil War Sites in the Eastern Theater

Civil War Sites in the South

Colorado's Mountains

Dallas & Fort Worth

Denver

El Paso

Florida Keys & Key West

Gettysburg

Glacier National Park

Great Smoky Mountains

Greater Fort Lauderdale

Greater Tampa Bay Area

Hampton Roads

Houston

Hudson River Valley

Indianapolis

Jacksonville

Kansas City

Long Island

Louisville

Madison

Maine Coast

Memphis

Myrtle Beach & the Grand Strand

Nashville

New Orleans

New York City

North Carolina's Mountains

North Carolina's Outer Banks

North Carolina's Piedmont Triad

Oklahoma City

Orange County, CA

Oregon Coast

Palm Beach County

Palm Springs

Philadelphia & Pennsylvania Dutch Country

Phoenix

Portland, Maine

Portland, Oregon

Raleigh, Durham & Chapel Hill

Richmond, VA

Reno and Lake Tahoe

St. Louis

San Antonio

Santa Fe

Savannah & Hilton Head

Seattle

Shreveport

South Dakota's Black Hills Badlands

Southwest Florida

Tucson

Tulsa

Twin Cities

Washington, D.C.

Williamsburg & Virginia's Historic Triangle

Yellowstone & Grand Teton

Yosemite

**To order call 800-243-0495
or visit www.Insiders.com**

 # Getaway ideas for the local traveler

Need a day away to relax, refresh, renew?
Just get in your car and go!

day trips®

from houston

>>>

getaway idea
laura nathan-ga

day trips®

from washington, d.c

>>>

getaway ideas for the local trave

day trips®

from orange county, ca

>>>

getaway ideas for the local trave

day trips®

from seattle

>>>

getaway ideas for the local trave
chloë ernst

day trips®

from dallas/fort worth

>>>

getaway ideas for the local traveler
sandra ramani

To order call 800-243-0495 or visit www.GlobePequot.com